PHILOSOPHY'S PLACE IN CULTURE

A Model

Mark D. Morelli

UNIVERSITY
PRESS OF
AMERICA

LANHAM • NEW YORK • LONDON

Copyright © 1984 by

University Press of America,™ Inc.

4720 Boston Way
Lanham, MD 20706

3 Henrietta Street
London WC2E 8LU England

Library of Congress Cataloging in Publication Data

Morelli, Mark D.
  Philosophy's place in culture.

  Bibliography: p.
  1. Culture–Philosophy. 2. Philosophy. I. Title.
HM101.M77   1984   306'.01   83–21707
ISBN 0–8191–3673–5 (alk. paper)
ISBN 0–8191–3674–3 (pbk. : alk. paper)

All University Press of America books are produced on acid-free
paper which exceeds the minimum standards set by the National
Historical Publications and Records Commission.

IN LOVING MEMORY OF MY FATHER

Dino A. Morelli
Chairman of the Department of Engineering Design
California Institute of Technology

1916 - 1972

ACKNOWLEDGEMENTS

I am very grateful to Professors T. D. Langan, T. M. Robinson, and E. A. Synan of the University of Toronto for their helpful comments on early drafts of the present essay. To my good friends, Hew Elcock and Deborah Schuller, I am indebted for their unselfish interest in this project and for their many valuable suggestions. I owe special thanks to Elizabeth Morelli. From start to finish, her incisive questions and keen insights have enlightened me, and her warm companionship has sustained me.

C O N T E N T S

x

PREFACE

My concern in what follows is to begin to carve out a cultural niche for philosophers. Philosophers reflect upon human endeavors in so peculiar a fashion as to appear virtually useless to the culture at large; lacking a clear account of their true value to culture, they embark on a variety of unflattering, self-protective maneuvers that serve to postpone indefinitely their deliberate and methodical intervention in culture.

Some light may be shed upon philosophy's present plight and its consequences for philosophic praxis by borrowing a distinction drawn by Richard Rorty between 'philosophy' and 'Philosophy'. While 'philosophy' is the pursuit of a synoptic view, a view of how things hang together, 'Philosophy', in its two dominant forms -- the 'empirical' and the 'transcendental' -- promotes a restricted view, after having made a near fatal distinction between mere opinion and genuine knowledge. [1] Although the distinction is interpreted differently by 'empiricists' and 'transcendentalists', it serves to block the attainment, by either form of 'Philosophy', of the synoptic view 'philosophy' would reach. It amounts to a pre-understanding, a prejudice, that things do not in fact hang together, that some things simply "hang out", as it were, and are to be removed altogether from the cultural scene or, at least, subjugated to some preferred human endeavor. As Rorty has noted, this distinction is invidious: it has 'empiricists' giving offense to 'transcendentalists' and vice versa, and it has both types giving offense to unphilosophical folks. But these offensive positions are self-protective ruses. 'Transcendental Philosophy', in its earliest manifestations, had to preserve itself in the face of the notable propensity (still easily discernible in our day) of ordinary people and poets and the modern equivalents of sophists to banish from the face of the earth any impediment to the smooth performance of practico-social life that resists

being brushed hastily aside. As Socrates gave offense
to Anytus, Lycon and Meletus -- a politician, an
orator, and a poet -- so 'transcendental Philosophy',
in its incipient stages, gave offense to the culture
at large. The distinction between 'Philosophic' Truth
and mere opinion, while reflecting (in my opinion)
a normative breakthrough formative of the entire
Western tradition of inquiry, was tainted from the
start by a protective purpose and constituted the
ground for an imperialistic totalization of the 'Philosophic' outlook, method, and objective. 'Empirical
Philosophy', on the other hand, in particular the
positivist tradition, has more recently given its
all to emerging modern science, appropriating to
the degree it could the natural scientific outlook,
method and object, and employing the distinction
between empirical Truth and 'nonsense' to bulwark
its threatened position. Whereas the 'transcendental'
side seeks to preserve itself as a cultural endeavor
by totalization, 'empirical Philosophy' seeks to
secure itself against the threat of elimination from
the cultural scene by capitulating to that human
endeavor that has achieved the status of cultural
ideal.

Now, these stratagems do indeed preserve for
philosophy a place in the cultural milieu; but the
'place' is hardly a 'niche'; that is to say, it is
hardly a position from which philosophers may operate
deliberately, methodically and effectively to influence the culture. Our culture could easily do without
'Philosophy', as separated as it is from its original
aspiration to achieve a synoptic view. But our culture,
I believe, cannot do without 'philosophy'; and, to
the degree these 'Philosophical' attempts at self-
preservation are recognized to be "holding actions",
preservative of some place, at least, for the original
philosophic aspiration, albeit in an imperfect and
distorted form, totalizing and capitulating 'Philosophy' may evoke our sympathy and, with appropriate
reservations, our approval. The problem facing us,
then, is not solved by imprecating a plague upon
both their houses, because their houses, while perhaps
constructed from the wrong set of plans, are home
to us as well. Rather, the project before us is one
of constructing a guiding vision of philosophy's
place in culture that at once discloses a niche that
philosophers might fearlessly and comfortably inhabit
and sheds light upon the defensive postures we have
been taking. In the present essay I shall attempt

xii

to expose the basic features of my vision of a worth-while cultural role for philosophers, a vision that is, I hope, free of invidious defensiveness.

Two far-reaching questions, then, determine the subject-matter and direction of this essay. First and foremost, what task may philosophers reasonably be called upon to perform in our culture? Is philosophy peculiarly suited for a specific function in the existing cultural matrix? Second, what is the present cultural situation? A correct answer to the first question presupposes a correct answer to the second; successful cultural self-orientation pre-supposes an understanding of the cultural situation.

These two questions are intricate. The contemporary cultural situation is highly complex; the proper role of philosophy has long been a matter for controversy. Accordingly, I shall not attempt to answer these questions fully in this short essay. I propose instead to undertake a preparatory maneuver, as it were, by attempting to construct a way of approaching determinate answers to these questions. I hope to shed light on the structure of cultural matrices in general, to expose typical features of cultural contexts of philosophic activity, and to indicate schematically the major, significant options confronting philosophers in our day.

As this study proceeds, numerous questions of related interest may emerge in the mind of the reader. But these questions, bearing upon such topics as the objectivity of judgments of fact and value, the differences between the various endeavors constitutive of our culture, and the ground of the unity of the various endeavors, need not be addressed here with great thoroughness and precision. The pursuit of answers to questions such as these does constitute partly the philosophic task; but their detailed treatment is not required by the purpose at hand. My aim is to equip the student of philosophy, notorious in non-philosophic circles for his inability to define unequivocally the nature of his discipline and its cultural role, with a broad view of his cultural position and the options it places before him. Nevertheless, it is hoped that the task of finding satisfactory answers to these important questions and others will have been made easier by my preparatory study and my schematic survey of the options confronting philosophers.

The essay is divided into four parts. In Chapter I I shall introduce a model of sufficient breadth for the fruitful investigation of relations between the various endeavors constitutive of a cultural matrix. The fruit of this chapter is the <u>horizonal structure</u> in its most basic and general form. Chapter II is divided into two parts. In the first part the horizonal structure is compared and contrasted with classificatory schemes of a basically sociological nature in order to promote a clear apprehension of the unfamiliar horizonal structure. In the second part I expose the philosophic presuppositions of the model and defend its heuristic adequacy by comparing and contrasting it with the ancient Aristotelian scheme of ways of life and with the modern scheme of sub-worlds devised by William James. In Chapter III I shall expose the main types of relations into which horizons may enter and distinguish different types of configurations of co-existing horizons. Finally, in Chapter IV, with the expanded model as a guide, I shall exhibit the major significant options confronting philosophers seeking to orientate themselves in their culture, and I shall use the expanded model to inform my account of the process of deliberation which the self-orientating philosopher may follow. In the final section of Chapter IV I shall propose a practical philosophic task which, I believe, effectively exploits the knowledge gained by philosophers to meet the demands of our present cultural situation.

FOOTNOTES TO THE PREFACE

[1]See Rorty's <u>Consequences of Pragmatism: Essays: 1972-1980</u> (Minneapolis: University of Minnesota Press, 1982), Introduction: Pragmatism and Philosophy.

There remain the philosophers, a group apart if ever
there was one, yet seemingly unsure of their function.
Some identify their cause with that of common sense
and ordinary language. Others assume the role of
spokesmen for science. Still others switch their
reflective concern to the hermeneutics of existence
and the originality of <u>Geschichte</u>. Greeks of old
sought to be universalist and autonomous by discoursing
on being. A few moderns take their cue from the differentiation of horizons by specialization and, through
an appeal to authentic subjectivity, seek to distinguish and evaluate the various orientations of the
polymorphic consciousness of man.

Bernard Lonergan

I

THE HORIZONAL STRUCTURE

The purpose of the present chapter is to assemble
the elements of a <u>model</u> which may be employed as
a heuristic device by students of culture and by
philosophers attempting to discover their place in
contemporary culture. Bernard Lonergan has succinctly
expressed the nature of a model.

> By a model is not meant something to be copied
> or imitated. By a model is not meant a description
> of reality or a hypothesis about reality. It is
> simply an intelligible, interlocking set of terms
> and relations that it may be well to have about
> when it comes to describing reality or to forming
> hypotheses. As the proverb, so the model is some-
> thing worth keeping in mind when one confronts
> a situation or tackles a job.[1]

The model whose elements are to be assembled is to
be of sufficient generality and yet of sufficient
determinacy to be useful as a guide both for the
investigation of cultural matrices and their internal
relations and for the orientation of philosophic
activity within any cultural matrix to which a philosopher might belong. On the one hand, the model is
to provide students of culture with a structured
anticipation of the types of dynamic relations possible within any cultural matrix of sufficient complexity. On the other hand, it is to provide philosophers with an appreciation of the broad context
of their activities which may render their conduct
more deliberate and methodical.

The model may be named the <u>horizonal structure</u>,
for the notion of <u>horizon</u> is the most important element of the model. The remaining basic elements of
the model are related to the central notion of horizon.

1

A _cultural matrix_ is a _structure_ whose elements are horizons. Horizons may be _ordinary_ or _extraordinary_. They may be present to their subjects and to other subjects of distinct horizons as _merely experienced_ or as _actually known_. In themselves, horizons are interlocked sets of _standpoints, modes of operation, and worlds_. The horizons of subjects are _expressed_ in language and artifacts. The horizons constituting our cultural matrix at the present time seem to number six: ordinary, _artistic_, _scientific_, _scholarly_, _philosophic_, and _religious_. Finally, in a single subject horizons may be _combined_. As these basic elements of the model are discussed, the horizonal structure in its most basic and general form will begin to take shape.

1. CULTURE

The notion of culture is central to the disciplines of cultural anthropology and philosophical anthropology. Two meanings of culture may be distinguished: (i) the classicist or axiological notion, and (ii) the empirical or objective notion.[2] The first meaning of culture is too determinate to be useful as a tool for the non-partisan investigation of relations composing cultural matrices. The second meaning, in turn, is too indeterminate or vague to be useful.

The classicist notion of culture was normative or axiological. It reflected the view that _de jure_ there was only one culture that was both universal and permanent.[3] Some states of human existence were thought to be cultured while others were uncultured. In this sense, culture is a positive goal equated with social progress.[4] In different historical periods, different ideals of culture in this sense have reigned: the literary ideal of Cicero and Quintilian; the theological ideals of Augustine and Thomas; the scientific ideal of Comte and the Encyclopaedists.[5] For the most part, this notion of culture has been displaced in scientific studies by the empirical notion, but its persistence in the background of recent anthropological thought is reflected by the recurrent use of pejorative categories such as 'savages' and 'primitives'.[6]

The modern notion of culture is empirical. A culture is a set of meanings and values that informs a way of life. The set may in fact remain the same for ages, acquiring a semblance of permanence, but it may also develop or decline.[7] In the modern anthropological sense, culture is a specific mode of activity of living beings and a specific mode of organization of their collective life.[8] The operative distinction in the past was between the cultured and barbarians. At present, the operative distinction is between the cultural activities of humans and those activities peculiar to purely biological forms.[9] Kroeber and Kluckhohn have formulated a summary definition of the notion of culture employed by American anthropologists at mid-century.

> Culture consists of patterns, explicit or implicit, of and for behavior acquired and transmitted by symbols constituting the distinctive achievement of human groups, including their embodiments in artifacts; the essential core of culture consists of traditional (i.e., historically derived and selected) ideas and especially their attached values; culture systems may, on the one hand, be considered as products of action, on the other, as conditioning elements of further action.[10]

While the classicist notion of culture is too determinate, the modern notion of culture is too indeterminate or broad. E. S. Markarian has recently complained that

> too broad a definition of culture as 'not nature' or 'creations of men' do not set the boundaries of the phenomenon, nor do they give a particular frame of reference for studying human activity. And it is this very problem which seems to be most interesting and complicated today in specifying the concept of culture.[11]

The modern notion of culture, while it points in the general direction of answers to the leading questions of this essay, is too broad to be a useful component of the model.[12] The model itself is to be a refinement of this notion of culture, giving the notion additional determinacy without transforming it back into the classicist notion.

Markarian has outlined the additional determinations which he believes are required to make the notion of culture an effective methodological tool. A rather lengthy summary of his requirements is called for, for they provide a foretaste of the notion of horizon which is central to the model being developed.

An integrated understanding of a society requires consideration from three different points of view: (1) the point of view of <u>the subjects of the activity</u>, in answer to the question <u>who is acting</u>; (2) the point of view of <u>the fields of activity</u>, in answer to the question <u>what are the objects and goals of human activity</u>; (3) the viewpoint of <u>the mode of activity</u>, in answer to the question <u>how, in which manner</u>, this human activity is implemented. Markarian believes that this approach to social reality — a three-dimensional one — makes it possible to embrace all the multiformity of human society and, as well, provides science with the criteria necessary for the classification of the elementary components of human society and for the distinction of its different structural sections and connections. The structural relations express (1) relations between human individuals and groups, (2) relations between various fields of socially-directed human activity, and (3) relations between all kinds of means of stimulation, regulation, programming, realization and reproduction of human activity derived extrabiologically. Finally, by abstracting these structural sections, Markarian believes, it is possible to distinguish three classes of elements encountered by the student of society. The first class embraces <u>the subject of human activity</u> in its various manifestations. The second class includes various <u>types and spheres of human activity</u>. The third class of elements includes <u>the diverse forms manifested by culture</u>.[13]

A three-dimensional approach to the study of culture will be the essential characteristic of the model. Its incorporation is demanded by the nature of the questions guiding the present essay. The ultimate question pertains to the philosopher's place and role in a culture; it pertains to the activity or conduct of a subject of a particular type. Consequently, the prior question regarding the existing situation cannot be focussed narrowly upon the "objective mind" or the "mind-affected world" considered simply as the artificial world and its configurations. Nor can it be focussed simply upon what Dilthey named "objectifications of life": "everything human beings have created and in which they have embodied their thoughts, feelings and intentions."[14] The prior question

4

must be directed towards objectifications of life, modes of objectification, and objectifiers. Without the incorporation of the three-dimensional approach, a model may still be valuable for investigators of "objective mind", but it will not be adequately determinate to guide philosophic conduct.

2. STRUCTURE

A cultural matrix is a dynamic structure. Bernard Lonergan has drawn a useful distinction between a whole, a structure, and a materially dynamic structure.[15] A conventional quantity or arbitrary collection whose parts are determined by a conventional or arbitrary division is a whole, but it is not a structure. The closed set of relations between such a whole and its parts is an "arbitrary jumble of arithmetic ratios." But some wholes are highly organized products of nature or art, and these wholes are different.

Then the set of internal relations is of the greatest significance. Each part is what it is in virtue of its functional relations to other parts; there is no part that is not determined by the exigences of other parts; and the whole possesses a certain inevitability in its unity, so that the removal of any part would destroy the whole, and the addition of any further part would be ludicrous. Such a whole is a structure.

Structures may be static or dynamic. A dynamic structure whose parts are activities is materially dynamic.[16]

A culture is a highly organized product of art that is at least materially dynamic. For, while the notion of culture includes artifacts, it also includes modes of activity and the subjects who produce the artifacts. Moreover, besides the dynamic relations between subjects and objects, both natural and artificial, and the relations of subjects to themselves, there are the dynamic relations of subjects to one another. A cultural matrix is a materially dynamic structure. The model to be developed must anticipate the structured dynamism of its object. It must be a structured anticipation of a whole constituted by activities which are intrinsically related to one another and to the whole. However, it is to be recalled that the model itself is just an abstract

set of terms and relations to be kept in mind by
students of culture and philosophers interested in
conducting themselves on the level of their time.

3. HORIZON

A culture may be conceived as a structure of
horizons.

The word 'horizon' is used commonly to signify
the apparent intersection of the earth and sky as
seen by an observer. "The sun is sinking below the
horizon." It is also employed in an analogous sense
to signify the range of an individual's knowledge,
experience, observation, and interests. "Mathematical
physics is completely beyond my horizon." I shall
employ the word in this analogous sense, with some
additional refinements.

In the analogous sense, a horizon includes not
only visible objects but also objects of knowledge
and objects and objectives of anticipation or interest. Objects of knowledge may be present or absent, possible or impossible. But a range is an area
or sphere in which any activity takes place. In its
analogous sense, a horizon includes more than objects
and objectives. It includes the activities of human
subjects as well. Subjects are conscious.[17] We know
and we anticipate, but we are also aware of knowing
and anticipating. If called upon to account for ourselves at any moment we may respond, "I was just
trying to figure something out" or "I was daydreaming"
or "I was studying". The range of objects and objectives of human subjects is not independent of the
standpoints and activities of human subjects, and
those standpoints and activities are more or less
fully within the horizons of subjects. A horizon
may include not only objects of observation, objects
of knowledge, and objects and objectives of interest
but also both the subject who observes, knows, and
anticipates and the activities of observing, knowing,
and anticipating. For the most part, objects other
than ourselves as subjects and our activities are
foci of interest and subject-matter of inquiry. But
we are also more or less fully within the range of
our knowledge and interest. The human subject, inasmuch as he is awake, is at least present to himself
or conscious, although he may not know himself in
a technical sense of 'knowing'. Hence the vagueness

of the illustrative expressions above may be a function, not of their lack of reference, but of unde-
veloped understanding of that to which they refer.
In Section 5 the accessibility of modes of operation
shall be considered.

In a refined analogous sense, then, a horizon
has three related components or aspects: a subject-
pole, an object-pole, and an active relation of sub-
ject-pole to object-pole. Any horizon may be considered under any or all of its three aspects. Considered as a subject, the horizon may be named a
standpoint. Considered as an object and an objective, it may be named a world. Considered as an affective and cognitive relation between a standpoint
and a world, it may be named a mode of operation.
A subject's mode of operation and standpoint may
be either a merely present or an actually known part
of his world. By definition, the three components
of any horizon are intrinsically related. A world
strictly implies a mode of operation and a standpoint.
Distinct worlds strictly imply distinct modes of
operation and standpoints.[18]

4. ORDINARY AND EXTRAORDINARY

Horizons may be divided initially into two major types to facilitate a grasp of the horizonal
structure of a culture. Some horizons are ordinary
and some are extraordinary. One may think of the
horizon of the man of common sense, on the one hand,
and of the horizon of intellectuals or men of ideas,
on the other. By 'extraordinary' I mean "beyond what
is ordinary, usual, or commonplace" rather than 'ex-
ceptional' or 'remarkable'. The latter terms are
employed, for example, to describe athletic feats.
In that employment they have a connotation of un-
matched superiority. However, I shall employ the
word 'extraordinary' with descriptive neutrality.
'Ordinary' is also to be employed without evaluative
connotations. By the ordinary horizon is meant the
usual human standpoint related to the usual human
world by the usual mode of operation. By an extraordinary horizon is meant an unusual human standpoint related to an unusual human world by an unusual
mode of operation.[19]

7

5. EXPERIENCE AND KNOWLEDGE

Every horizon, as human, is present to itself or conscious; it has a self-taste, as it were.[20] If confusion is to be avoided, a distinction must be made between self-presence and self-knowledge. The distinction has its precedent in successful scientific performance. As gaping and gazing are distinguished from scientific observation, as looking-for and looking-at are distinguished from scientific scrutiny, so self-presence may be distinguished from advertence to oneself as a conscious subject, and self-experience may be distinguished from self-attention. As scientific observation and description are distinguished from scientific explanation and theorizing, so advertence to oneself as a conscious subject may be distinguished from understanding oneself as a conscious subject. As scientific theories in general are distinguished from those particular theories which ground successful scientific predictions, so self-understanding may be distinguished from adequate self-knowledge.[21] If these distinctions are allowed, then it follows that at any time only some horizons may be expected to have advanced beyond self-presence to understand and judge themselves as standpoints, worlds, and modes of operation. As human development, so horizonal development is a process of learning. Through the learning process a horizon is constituted. Some subjects know themselves as horizons, but others are merely self-present or in process of coming to know themselves as horizons. We may distinguish between horizons of experience, including self-present modes of operation and standpoints as experienced, and horizons of self-knowledge which are constituted by inquiry into oneself as present. The horizon of experience of an extraordinary subject includes the horizon of experience of an ordinary subject, but the reverse is not true.

As horizons are at the very least self-present, so they are present to one another inasmuch as human life is also social life. Some subjects have advanced beyond mere consciousness of the Other to understand and judge the Other as standpoint, world, and mode of operation. Some subjects have advanced only so far as the formulation of a possible understanding of the Other as standpoint, world, and mode of operation, or simply as world, simply as standpoint, simply as mode of operation. For the most part, it seems, horizons are merely present to one another, having no carefully elaborated mutual understanding.

8

This is especially true of the mutual presence of ordinary and extraordinary horizons.[22]

6. STANDPOINT, MODE OF OPERATION, WORLD

A standpoint is a position from which things are judged and courses of action are settled upon and carried out. It is the locus of a coalescence of judgments into the context named a mentality and also the locus of a guiding set of values and ideals.[23] It is he or she who knows and decides inasmuch as he or she is informed by personally-generated knowledge, by the group's beliefs, by reasonable decisions and deliberate conduct, by the decisions of others and traditional ideals. As a standpoint is a symbiosis of knowledge and belief, so one may speak of the standpoint of the group, the group mentality.[24] As it is also a function of personal and group orientations, so one may speak of the group ideal.

A world is that which is apprehended from a particular standpoint. It is the object-pole of a horizon, but it is objective not in an absolute sense but only in a relative sense. It is the field of objects experienced, understood, or known by a subject, and also that field of objects and objectives to which a subject is related affectively as merely interested, somewhat interested, very interested, or disaffected. Among the objects in the field is the subject himself as at least present to himself as experiencing, understanding, judging, deciding and as feeling.[25] A world may be partially coincident with some part or aspect of the universe of being and the truly good, but it need not be. The horizonal self-understanding of a subject may be incorrect, giving rise to a variety of distortions of his standpoint and mode of operation.

A mode of operation is the affective and cognitive relation of a standpoint to a world. As there are many horizons, but only one human nature ex hypothesi, we may distinguish between surface modes of operation and a deep mode. Surface modes vary from horizon to horizon; they assume their dynamic forms as standpoints are constituted and worlds take shape. By the deep mode is meant something akin to what Lonergan has named the invariant dynamic structure of cognitional activity, or transcendental method, or what Newman has named the organum investigandi, or what Apel alludes to when he speaks of a notion of science "that is relevant to the philosophy and methodology of science, and that, none the less, is not restricted to the 'logic of science'."[26] It is the common general form shared more or less completely by every surface mode of operation. Every subject experiences, understands, judges, and decides. As a rule, questions are preceded by experience, understandings are preceded by questions, judgments are preceded by reflective questions, and decisions are preceded by deliberative questions. But in every case the experiences that are questioned, the questions that are asked, and the hypotheses and courses of action that are proposed arise in consciousness in a context determined by a mentality. As contexts vary, so surface modes of operation vary within the broad limits imposed by the deep mode or general form that is common, on the one hand, and by individual and social habits which lead to either the omission of one or more moments of the deep mode or inadequately thorough implementation of the deep mode.

7. EXPRESSION

A cultural matrix is constituted by ordinary and extraordinary expression. By 'expression' is meant 'manifestation', that which communicates, indicates, embodies, or symbolizes something. Subjects speak, write, compose, build, design, institute. Their language, writings, compositions, constructions, inventions, and institutions reflect the variety of horizons. Some ordinary linguistic expression is about extraordinary horizons, and some extraordinary expression is about the ordinary horizon. As horizons are, for the most part, merely present to one another, having no carefully elaborated mutual understanding, expressions about horizons normally do not take the form of theories, explanations, definitions, or explicit positions. One horizon's expression about another normally takes the form of an allusion, an indirect but pointed and meaningful reference. In those cases where reference is more direct and overt, it is also most often evaluative rather than descriptive, expressing a judgment of value that has been added to a foregone intellectual conclusion. However, there are some subjects who make it their business to understand the full range of horizons and whose expression about horizons takes the form of intentionally neutral descriptions.

A _horizon_ is a _self-present_ and possibly _self-knowing_ _standpoint_, _mode of operation_, and _world_. It may be _ordinary_ or _extraordinary_. It _expresses_ itself, and some of its expressions are allusions to other horizons. A _culture_ may be conceived as a materially dynamic _structure_ of horizons. The question now arises, How many horizons are there? This set of terms must be supplemented by an additional set towards the completion of the account of the basic elements of the horizonal structure.

8. THE NUMBER AND KINDS OF HORIZONS

The number and kinds of horizons may be revealed by means of a linguistic reflection guided by the notion of horizon that has been developed. I shall consider words and phrases in common use. By "common use" is not meant "ordinary use". Analysis of ordinary language is too limiting when we are concerned to discover the _full range_ of existing standpoints, modes of operation, and worlds. By "common use" is meant "general use". So it is that a first approximation to the determination of the number and kinds of horizons may be obtained by adverting to the distinction between the ordinary horizon and a set of extraordinary horizons. This distinction is commonly employed, although usually in terms that are evaluative and therefore useless in the present context. The nature of the distinction will become apparent as the linguistic reflection proceeds. However, it should be noted at the outset that the lists of words and phrases that are assembled here are illustrative and not exhaustive. They are intended to facilitate an identification of the distinct horizons and a determination of their number.

8.1 ORDINARY STANDPOINT

Extraordinary subjects, those who are not simply men of common sense, employ a variety of words and phrases to designate the _ordinary standpoint in its singularity_: the plain man, the vulgar man, the man of experience, the man of the natural standpoint, the average man, the common man, the practical man, the man of sound judgment, the man of common sense, the layman, the man of sense, etc. Another collection is employed by extraordinary subjects to designate the _ordinary standpoint in its plurality_: the crowd, the herd, the multitude, the masses, the public,

11

the people, the great unwashed, the common people, etc. The frequency with which these words and phrases are employed by extraordinary subjects varies with the historical period under consideration. "The vulgar man" was more common in Hume's time than it is at present, while "the masses" occurs today with notable frequency and was not used in Hume's time.[27] Moreover, different connotations are attached to these words and phrases in different historical periods, and these connotations reflect relations between horizons. In Roman times the vulgus were the common people, but today 'vulgar' means not only unrefined but also ignorant, rude and offensive. Many extraordinary expressions alluding to the ordinary standpoint have evaluative connotations, and these connotations are normally pejorative subsequent to the period of Enlightenment.

8.2. ORDINARY WORLD

Extraordinary subjects employ another collection of words and phrases to designate the world of the ordinary horizon: the mundane, the life-world, trivia, the routine, everyday life, the practical realm, the realm of human affairs, the world of experience, the sensible world, the domain of common sense, etc. In their extraordinary employment certain of these words and phrases also have evaluative connotations. The mundane and the routine are not only uninteresting to the extraordinary subject as a rule, but they are considered to be positively distracting as well.

8.3. ORDINARY MODE OF OPERATION

Still another collection of words and phrases is used by extraordinary subjects to indicate the ordinary mode of operation: know-how, experience,[28] sound judgment, good sense, bon sens, gesunder Menschenverstand, native intelligence, everyday thinking, practical sense, experiencing, sensing, natural inference, motherwit, etc. Designations of the ordinary mode of operation are commonly found to have positive connotations.

8.4. AMBIGUITY AND THE ORDINARY MODE

Words and phrases employed by extraordinary subjects to designate the ordinary mode of operation

12

exhibit a significant ambiguity not shared by those found in the previous lists. We say that one should use one's common sense; but we also say that one should have common sense. The same ambiguity inheres in 'know-how', 'experience', 'sound judgment', 'good sense', 'bon sens', 'gesunder Menschenverstand', 'native intelligence', and 'practical sense'. The ambiguity may be traced provisionally to two sources, although a more detailed analysis would be required to account completely for the ambiguity.

First, there is a difficulty inherent in any attempt to give expression to the ordinary mode of operation. The ordinary mode is subtle and versatile. For example, the trouble-shooter cannot put his know-how into a pamphlet for others to read and simply follow; he must travel to the spot, and those who accompany him learn his trade by apprenticeship. Again, the doctor must see the patient before making a diagnosis and a lawyer must know the facts of a particular case before entering a plea. The ordinary mode is not deliberately methodical in the manner of modern empirical science; it is spontaneous.[29]

In the second place, the ordinary mode is to a great extent habitual. Problematic situations tend to recur in everyday life; dealing with these similar situations soon becomes "a matter of course". Habits are difficult to break and difficult to articulate. If a habit is to be broken, it must first be articulated; but to give expression to a habit, to objectify it, requires deliberate and thoughtful expression of that which, because habitual, occurs without deliberation and thought.[30] The ordinary mode is obscured from view by a familiarity bred of repetition.

The recurrence of the word 'sense' in extraordinary expression of the ordinary mode is related to the first source of ambiguity, the subtle versatility of the ordinary mode of operation. In this employment, 'sense' does not mean 'meaning' as in the expression, "'Two plus two is very funny' doesn't make sense." Nor does it have the meaning 'sense' has in the expression, "He lost his sense of smell." It has the significance of 'sense' found in the following expressions: "He has no sense of propriety"; "He doesn't have the good tracker's sense"; "He has no sense of humor."

The latency of the connotation of activity or operation, which may lead one to believe that there is no extraordinary acknowledgement of the existence of an ordinary mode of operation, is related to the second source of ambiguity, the habitual nature of the ordinary mode of operation. Habitual operations go unnoticed for the most part, that is, except when they become irrelevant to the situation at hand. That which can be done whenever one pleases, without thinking, requires no unusual effort of attention.

The words and phrases employed by extraordinary subjects to designate the ordinary mode of operation, then, are ambiguous; but their ambiguity may be accounted for by adverting to the habitual and situation-specific character of ordinary operation. The expressions, despite their ambiguity, do point to an ordinary mode of operation, an active relation between standpoint and world.

8.5. THE SET OF EXTRAORDINARY STANDPOINTS

Both ordinary and extraordinary subjects employ words and phrases to designate the whole set of extraordinary standpoints: intellectuals, intelligentsia, intellectual elite, the cultured,[31] the educated, the over-educated, 'brains', the refined, know-it-alls, les clercs, speculators, dreamers, men of ideas, thinkers, men of learning, scholars, researchers, savants, sophists, academicians, academics, professors, absent-minded professors, ivory-tower intellectuals, idealists, etc. As the recurrence of 'sense' in extraordinary expression of the ordinary mode is related to the subtle versatility of ordinary operation, so the recurrence of a family of words connoting a concerted effort of learning is related to the extraordinary point of view.

8.6. EXTRAORDINARY WORLDS

There does not appear to be a single collection of related words and phrases commonly employed to designate a single world shared by the set of extraordinary standpoints. While the ordinary world is commonly assumed to be one, provided we prescind from differences rooted in psychological aberrations and physical dysfunctions, extraordinary worlds are commonly assumed to be many.

8.6.1. THE UNITY OF THE ORDINARY WORLD

The ordinary world is assumed to be one in spite
of the commonplace that each man lives in a world
of his own. This commonplace is employed by the ordinary subject in several ways. It is used to account
for minor differences of taste or preference. It
is used to "explain away" impractical or inappro-
priate divergences from conventional routine, or
to remove the threat to order perceived to originate
from the existence of such divergences. It is used
as a way of accounting for the idiosyncracies of
behavior and expression that attend an acknowledged
and welcomed multiplicity of personalities and to
lessen the monotony of many an ordinary endeavor.
The commonplace is not employed to deny the uniqueness
of the ordinary world. As a unique world strictly
implies a unique standpoint, so, as we have seen,
the ordinary standpoint is commonly taken to be one.

8.6.2. A MULTIPLICITY OF EXTRAORDINARY WORLDS

A collection of related words and phrases is
employed ordinarily to designate extraordinary standpoints considered as a set. Apparently, these standpoints cannot be accounted for by appealing to variations in temperamental disposition. An appeal to
temperament may be made to account for the ability
to maintain the strictly disciplined life of an extraordinary subject (e.g., that of the ascetic mystic),
but temperamental disposition is not cited ordinarily
to account for the emergence of the extraordinary
horizon itself. More than temperamental inclination
is required to make an intellectual, as ordinary
and extraordinary lamentations over wasted talent
suggest. Again, extraordinary horizons cannot be
"explained away" as intermittent and short-lived
divergences from the ordinary routine. Each extraordinary horizon is recognized to be extraordinary
because it involves a prolonged divergence from the
ordinary routine which occurs independently of variations in personality. Finally, it is also true that
each extraordinary subject lives in a world of his
own. But, as in the case of the ordinary subject,
this personal world is, as it were, a sub-world within
the world of the horizon. Does the ordinary reference
to extraordinary standpoints as a set imply that
there is only one extraordinary standpoint and only
one extraordinary world?

Both extraordinary and ordinary subjects acknowledge a <u>multiplicity of extraordinary worlds</u>. The
ordinary subject does not expect to hear identical
'stories' when he sits down first with "an Einstein"
and then with "a Rembrandt" or some other type of
extraordinary subject. But words and phrases designating these many worlds specifically and with relative precision are usually found in extraordinary
expression. Extraordinary subjects formulate sets
of designations for their respective worlds. Some
do this more explicitly than others. Some make it
their business to carry out this task of formulation.
The clarity and thoroughness of these extraordinary
self-references are dependent upon the degree and
extent of self-knowledge, a self-knowledge that results from inquiring exploitation of self-presence.
Moreover, sharing as they do the distinction of being
extraordinary, these subjects reflect to some degree
upon the remaining extraordinary horizons. Like seems
to seek like in cases where both instances of like-
ness are unusual. There is a fundamental truth imperfectly reflected by ordinary references to extraordinary worlds and standpoints as a <u>set</u>. Extraordinary
subjects read and appreciate with greater or less
attentiveness, interest, understanding, sympathy,
and completeness the writings and other productions
of other extraordinary subjects.[32] Consequently, designations such as the following may be found for a
<u>variety of extraordinary worlds</u>: the world of ideas,
the world of art, the world of literature, the world
of language, the drama of history, the world of science, the spiritual world, the material world, the
physical world, the natural world, the supernatural
world, etc. It is to be noted that as designations
become more precise and specific their number de-
creases, for they are normally found only in extraordinary expression and then only as a consequence
of a concerted effort of reflection.

8.6.3. THE PROBLEM OF THE IDENTITY OF WORLDS

The preceding collection of words and phrases
pertains to extraordinary worlds. How does the known
material world of an extraordinary horizon differ
from the known sensible world of the ordinary horizon?
A similar question may be posed with regard to other
pairs of designations, but the discussion of this
single question will suffice. It is to be noted that
the question pertains to the identity of worlds considered apart from their self-present dimensions.

This is an important qualification, for if it is overlooked the question may be taken to seek the differences between modes of operation and standpoints as self-present.

The question is an extraordinary one. In particular, it is a philosophic question. But it is a misleading philosophic question. A world is not independent of a mode of operation and a standpoint. Accordingly, confusion is avoided if the question is appropriately transformed. Is the material world to which the scientist as such is actively related the same as the sensible world to which the ordinary subject as such is actively related? The two worlds are not the same. While the ordinary subject may see a threatening bug, the entymologist may see something about which he could write a technical tome. While the lawyer in a courtroom may see the legal process at work, the behavioral psychologist may see a patterned sequence of stimuli and responses. While Eddington, the ordinary subject, may see a desk, the extraordinary, scientific Eddington may see mostly empty space.

The ambiguity of the word 'see' in these examples strengthens rather than weakens their illustrative significance. The ambiguity reflects a difference of standpoint and mode of operation. Different worlds strictly imply different standpoints and modes of operation. The word 'see', used in this manner, is radically ambiguous and obscure; it is a mere placeholder for a variety of expressions of possible, precise understandings of modes of operation and standpoints.

A further question arises. Aren't these two worlds the same world in some sense? The word 'world' as employed here is also ambiguous. The ambiguity can be eliminated and the latent presence of another meaning revealed if one asks instead, Are these two worlds the same universe of being? This philosophic question is extremely significant, but it cannot be treated here. Its solution is a necessary condition of any integration of the variety of horizons in a single, synoptic view, but my present concern is the identification of the variety of horizons and not their intellectual unification. The problem of the identity of worlds will acquire renewed significance later in this essay when I turn to the question of the task of philosophers in the existing horizonal situation.

17

8.6.4. ORDINARY APPREHENSION OF EXTRAORDINARY WORLDS

The ordinary subject, while apprehending obscurely the ties that bind extraordinary subjects, still recognizes the existence of a multiplicity of extraordinary worlds and standpoints. This recognition is reflected by ordinary expectations. Scientists and mystics are all unusual, but they are unusual in different ways. The ordinary subject may listen attentively to a mystic for hours, but he may doze off quickly at a lecture on mathematical physics.

Despite this recognition of extraordinary multiplicity, the ordinary subject normally designates extraordinary worlds as a set and by negation. Extraordinary standpoints are ordinarily said to be concerned with the abstract, the ideal, the irrelevant, the impractical, the useless, the boring, while the ordinary standpoint is said to be concerned with the concrete, the real, the relevant, the practical, the useful, and the interesting. While advertence to these negative characterizations does not contribute much to the determination of the number and kinds of horizons, their employment does reflect a significant deficiency in the ordinary ability to apprehend extraordinary subjects. Any extraordinary horizon is beyond the ordinary horizon. Extraordinary self-presence is not ordinary self-presence. On the other hand, because there do exist extraordinary designations for the ordinary standpoint, world, and mode of operation, the ordinary horizon may be assumed to be within an extraordinary world at least as an experienced horizon. Ordinary self-knowledge is accessible to extraordinary subjects, for ordinary self-presence is in some sense preserved in extraordinary self-presence. Consequently, there is no contradiction involved in speaking of Eddington, a well-known scientist, as both an ordinary subject and an extraordinary subject.

The presence, in some sense, of the ordinary horizon within every extraordinary horizon is a condition for the emergence of the philosophic problem of the identity of worlds. If there were not single subjects with more than one horizon, the problem would not arise. The problem is an extraordinary one. While ordinary subjects do recognize extraordinary multiplicity, they do not affirm the principle

18

that states that a multiplicity of extraordinary standpoints strictly implies a multiplicity of extraordinary worlds. Consequently, they do not anticipate the existence of extraordinary worlds and state that fact clearly. Rather, they only acknowledge a multiplicity obscurely in their performance, and they are content to characterize extraordinary worlds by negation. Those subjects who formulate principles relevant to ordinary and extraordinary human endeavors, among other things, are extraordinary subjects. Later in this essay, the significance of the ordinary horizon as the preserved starting-point of extraordinary endeavors will be considered further.[33]

8.7. EXTRAORDINARY MODES OF OPERATION

Both extraordinary and ordinary subjects employ words designating <u>extraordinary modes of operation</u>: (i) creating, dreaming, painting, philosophizing, musing, drawing, poetizing; (ii) thinking, studying, theorizing, dissecting, systematizing, analyzing, investigating, experimenting, hypothesizing, verifying, measuring; (iii) speculating, thinking, intellectualizing, hair-splitting, contemplating, studying, analyzing, synthesizing, clarifying, elucidating; (iv) interpreting, scholarship, studying, hair-splitting, researching, translating, investigating, theorizing, hypothesizin; (v) praying, philosophizing, meditating, preaching, worshiping, testifying, proselytizing; etc. Many of these words have pejorative connotations when employed by ordinary subjects. On the other hand, when used by extraordinary subjects to refer to one another, they have pejorative and laudatory connotations.

I have organized these words into groups. Some of the words listed occur in more than one group. Scientists, philosophers and scholars all study. Scientists and philosophers systematize and theorize. Philosophers and scholars, seen from the ordinary standpoint, "split hairs." The organization of the groups is not merely arbitrary. While some of the member words occur in more than one group, others belong in different groups. For example, 'painting', 'experimenting', 'synthesizing', 'interpreting', and 'praying' commonly are not used indiscriminately to refer to extraordinary modes of operation. They are employed by ordinary and extraordinary subjects alike to refer to different extraordinary modes of operation. However, they are employed by ordinary

19

subjects with less discrimination. Any theory, whether scientific or philosophic, may be named an interpretation by ordinary subjects, for example. 'Philosophizing' is ordinarily used to designate not only the mode of operation of the philosopher but also on occasion the modes of the poet, the mystic, and even the ordinary subject himself in his more reflective, less pragmatic moments. On the other hand, extraordinary subjects commonly acknowledge that the artist and the mystic normally do not philosophize, that the scientist does not create his object in the manner of the artist, that the mystic does not systematize, that scholars interpret while natural scientists do not, that scientists verify while artists do not, and so on.

8.8. EXTRAORDINARY STANDPOINTS

As expressions of extraordinary modes of operation fall into five groups, so there are five words commonly employed to designate <u>extraordinary standpoints</u>: artists, scientists, scholars, philosophers, religious.

8.9. RECAPITULATION

A brief summary of the results of the analysis is in order. A distinction is commonly made between the ordinary horizon, on the one hand, and extraordinary horizons considered as a set, on the other. Extraordinary subjects employ designations of the ordinary standpoint in its singularity and in its plurality, designations of the ordinary world, and designations of the ordinary mode of operation. Both ordinary and extraordinary subjects employ designations of extraordinary standpoints considered as a set, and both fail to designate precisely a single extraordinary world. Extraordinary subjects distinguish between extraordinary worlds and employ appropriate designations, while ordinary subjects designate extraordinary worlds as a set and by negation. Both extraordinary and ordinary subjects employ designations of extraordinary modes of operation, but ordinary subjects employ these with less discrimination.

8.10. THE NUMBER AND KINDS OF HORIZONS

At the outset it was laid down that, by definition, distinct worlds imply distinct standpoints
and modes of operation, and distinct modes of operation and standpoints imply distinct worlds. What
was originally an abstract proposition has been con-
cretized by a reflection upon general usage. Again,
in the refined analogous sense of 'horizon', a horizon is a self-present and possibly self-knowing standpoint, mode of operation, and world of a subject.
The existence of horizons is implicitly affirmed
by common linguistic usage. The question arises,
What are the standpoints, worlds, and modes of operation that have emerged and how great is their number,
as reflected imprecisely by common linguistic usage? The
following six terms provide the beginnings of an
answer: the ordinary horizon (the man in the street,
the layman, the man of common sense, etc.), the artistic horizon (painters, poets, composers, playwrights,
novelists, etc.), the scientific horizon (physicists,
chemists, biologists, psychologists, sociologists,
anthropologists, etc.), the scholarly horizon (men
of letters, critics, translators, historians, exe-
getes, interpreters, etc.), the philosophic horizon
(philosophers of natural science, of human studies,
of culture, metaphysicians, epistemologists, ethi-
cians, etc.), and the religious horizon (holy men
and women, mystics, saints, etc.).[34]

At the present time, it appears that six types
of horizon constitute the cultural matrix. These
six sets of standpoints, modes of operation, and
worlds are basic elements of the horizonal structure.
The six types have not been revealed by a transcendental deduction of categories; they happen to be
revealed by common linguistic usage. More types may
emerge in the future; fewer types may have existed
in the past. Moreover, the linguistic data could
also be arranged differently by investigators before
the model is employed. However, the linguistic evidence for the present division of types is strong,
and the same or similar divisions have been employed
by several thinkers concerned to organize and integrate
human endeavors.[35]

21

9. COMBINATIONS OF HORIZONS

A discussion of possible combinations of horizons in a single subject will virtually complete preparations for an exposition, in Chapter III, of the relations constitutive of groups of horizons. Possible combinations of horizons in single subjects are exposed here for two reasons. First, a problem arose regarding the relation of the ordinary horizon to any extraordinary horizon in a single subject. A deficiency in the ability of ordinary subjects to apprehend extraordinary subjects was noted. Any extraordinary horizon is beyond the ordinary horizon, but ordinary self-knowledge is accessible to extraordinary subjects. The presence of the ordinary horizon within every extraordinary horizon was said to be a necessary condition of the emergence of the philosophic problem of the identity of worlds. A discussion of combinations of horizons in single subjects, then, is required to accommodate these facts. Second, constellations of horizons are complex structures, but my exposition of horizonal relations will be schematic, focussing upon general types of relations and groups. An exposition which reflected the real complexity of cultural matrices would be so long that it would obscure the dynamic features I mean to expose. But a schematic study will suffice only if one can rest assured that its abstractness will not obscure the real complexity of the subject-matter in the very attempt to facilitate investigations. A review of the possible combinations of horizons in single subjects is offered in the interest of concreteness.

9.1. THE UNITY OF THE SUBJECT

A possible misunderstanding must first be noted. To speak of a single subject with more than one horizon is not to deny the unity of the single subject. If I were employing the analogous notion of horizon, without the refinements added early in this chapter, I could be accused of undermining the unity of the subject. For, in the analogous sense, a horizon is the limit of one's range of knowledge and interests, and more than one horizon would imply more than one limited range. Any extraordinary subject, then, would constitute subject-matter for a case-study of multiple personalities, and the unity of an extraordinary horizon would become a pressing problem. In the analogous sense of 'horizon', every subject has only one horizon. However, in the refined analogous sense, emphasis is not placed exclusively upon the world of the subject, the range of knowledge and interests, but upon the interconnected set of components -- world, standpoint, and mode of operation. An extraordinary subject is one who is capable of operating successfully in more than one mode, from more than one standpoint, with apprehensions of more than one world. To speak of a single subject with more than one horizon is not to undermine the unity of the subject. It is a more precise way of saying, for example, that a single man is both a good scientist and a good artist. In the refined analogous sense of 'horizon', any subject may have as many as six horizons, while remaining a single subject.

Because the attribution of more than one horizon to a single subject may generate confusion, in virtue of the familiarity of the analogous notion of horizon, I shall adopt the following convention. In cases where two horizons are combined in a single subject, I shall employ the extraordinary designation. For example, a single subject who is both ordinary and scientific shall be said to have a scientific horizon; a single subject who is both ordinary and religious shall be said to have a religious horizon. This convention actually serves two purposes. Besides mitigating the confusion that could be generated by the importation of the more familiar notion of horizon, it will serve to underline the fact, to be discussed in the next subsection, that every extraordinary horizon includes and goes beyond the ordinary horizon.

9.2. ORDINARY HORIZON AS PRESERVED STARTING-POINT

The ordinary horizon is a necessary precondition of the emergence of extraordinary endeavors. Every human subject must be a practical subject with greater or less regularity if he is to survive to pursue extraordinary ends. Every human subject must also be a dramatic or social subject with greater or less regularity, for human life is social life. The frequency and extent of ordinary practical operation requisite for the emergence and preservation of extraordinary endeavor may vary with different historical periods. But some frequency of recurrence of practical operations, and some duration of practical involvement are required for the maintenance of life. The frequency and extent of ordinary social operation may also

23

vary with different social situations and historical periods. But some frequency of recurrence of social interaction, and some duration of social involvement are required for the development of psychological integrity and linguistic facility.[36]

The ordinary horizon is not a sufficient precondition of the emergence of an extraordinary horizon. With the emergence of an extraordinary horizon, extraordinary ends displace practical and dramatic ends, extraordinary modes of operation displace the ordinary mode, extraordinary apprehensions of the universe of being displace the ordinary apprehension. This displacement is not an elimination. The theoretic ideal, for example, does not eliminate the practical ideal, but the practical ideal is held in abeyance by subjects who are operating theoretically. The emergence of theoretical operation, the pursuit of definitions in the manner of Aristotle, does not eliminate the need for practical operation, but practical operation is transcended or gone beyond by the theoretical subject as such. The emergence of the theoretical world apprehended by scientists does not eliminate the ordinary world apprehended by ordinary subjects, but that ordinary world is of little concern to the scientific subject as such. The ordinary horizon is not eliminated once and for all, but it is displaced temporarily in virtue of its being deliberately denied dominant status by a given subject. If the ordinary horizon were a sufficient precondition of extraordinary emergence, then extraordinary ideals, modes of operation, and worlds would be identical fundamentally with the ordinary ideal, mode, and world. But this identity is denied by ordinary linguistic performance. Ordinary designations of extraordinary horizons by negation imply difference, and these designations would not be formulated negatively if ordinary subjects were able to recognize their ideal and mode of operation, even obscurely, in the expression and performance of extraordinary subjects. The ordinary horizon is a necessary precondition of the emergence of extraordinary horizons, but it is not a sufficient precondition. Extraordinary horizons preserve but nevertheless go beyond the ordinary horizon.

9.3. COMBINATIONS

There is one type of horizon which is not combined with another horizon: the ordinary horizon.

24

There are five types of horizon which result from the combination of two horizons: the scientific, the artistic, the scholarly, the philosophic, and the religious horizon. These are the extraordinary horizons that have been mentioned to this point. They are the basic combinations of horizons in single subjects. Along with the ordinary horizon, these five will be central to the schematic study of the dynamic features of constellations of horizons. I shall turn, in Chapter III, to a consideration of the types of relations into which these six horizons enter.

Besides the ordinary horizon and the five basic combinations, there may be more complex combinations. With the five basic combinations additional extra-ordinary horizons may be combined. The mathematically possible combinations may be noted: ten cases of double combination, ten cases of triple combination, five cases of fourfold combination, and one case of fivefold combination. It should be noted, first, that these combinations pertain to single subjects; and, second, that they are only the mathematically possible combinations of horizons in single subjects.[37]

NOTES TO CHAPTER I

[1] Bernard Lonergan, Method in Theology (New York: Herder and Herder, 1972), xii.

[2] Ibid., xi. See also, E. S. Markarian, "The Concept of Culture in the System of Modern Sciences," in The Concept and Dynamics of Culture, ed. Bernardo Bernardi (The Hague; Paris: Moulton Publishers, 1977), pp. 103-118, especially pp. 103-104. Markarian distinguishes the 'axiological' notion from the 'objective' notion of culture, while Lonergan distinguishes the 'classicist' notion from the 'empirical' notion. Lonergan's terminology is preferable here. To call the empirical notion objective is to complicate the distinction enormously by importing an entire epistemology.

[3]Lonergan, Method in Theology, xi.

[4]Markarian, "The Concept of Culture in the System of Modern Sciences," in The Concept and Dynamics of Culture, p. 103.

[5]See Otto Bird, Cultures in Conflict: An Essay in the Philo-

25

sophy of the Humanities (Notre Dame; London: University of Notre Dame Press, 1976), Chaps. 1-3.

[6] Ikenna Nzimiro, "Anthropologists and Their Terminologies," in The Concept and Dynamics of Culture, pp. 503-520, especially pp. 509-513 on the notions of 'savages' and 'primitives'. The classicist notion continues to function in ordinary thinking about man more explicitly; but it is also being displaced gradually due to the combined influences of technological developments affecting travel and communication and the sedimentation of results of sociological and anthropological studies.

[7] Lonergan, Method in Theology, xi.

[8] Markarian, "The Concept of Culture in the System of Modern Sciences," in The Concept and Dynamics of Culture, p. 106.

[9] Ibid., p. 104.

[10] Alfred L. Kroeber and Clyde Kluckhohn, Culture: A Critical Review of Concepts and Definitions. Harvard University Peabody Museum of American Archeology and Ethnology Papers, Vol. 47, No. 1 (Cambridge, Mass.: The Museum, 1952), p. 181. See also, Milton Singer, "The Concept of Culture," International Encyclopaedia of the Social Sciences, ed. D. L. Sills (New York: Macmillan; The Free Press, 1968), pp. 527-543. Also, Christopher Dawson, The Age of the Gods (London, New York: Sheed & Ward, 1933), xiii-xvi. Dawson's is an early expression of the modern notion, similar to that of Lonergan. Hannah Arendt has discussed the Roman and Greek roots of the modern notion of culture in Between Past and Future: Eight Exercises in Political Thought (New York: The Viking Press, 1961), pp. 211-226. Her discussion of the notions of cultura anima and paideia brings clearly to light the axiological nature of the classicist notion.

[11] Markarian, "The Concept of Culture in the System of Modern Sciences," in The Concept and Dynamics of Culture, p. 104.

[12] See Clyde Kluckholn, "Anthropology in the Twentieth Century," in The Evolution of Science, eds. Guy S. Metraux and Francois Crouzet (Toronto: The New American Library of Canada Limited, 1963), p. 408: "Theory in cultural anthropology (apart from linguistics) is still rudimentary, except in the field of social organization. Culture, the central concept, is still somewhat amorphous."

[13] The ideas summarized here may be found in greater detail in "The Concept of Culture in the System of Modern Sciences," in The Concept and Dynamics of Culture, pp. 107-108.

[14] See the discussion by F. Allan Hanson, "Meaning in Culture,"

in The Concept and Dynamics of Culture, p. 252. The term "objectifications of life" is meant to include styles of life, forms
of social intercourse, a society's system of purposes, customs,
law, state, religion, art, science, and philosophy. While this
notion is broad, it is too emphatically objective. See Wilhelm
Dilthey, Pattern and Meaning in History, ed. H. P. Rickman (New
York: Harper and Row, 1962), p. 114, and Max Weber, The Theory
of Social and Economic Organization, trans. and eds. Talcott
Parsons and A. M. Henderson (New York: Oxford University Press,
1947), p. 93. On Dilthey's notion of objectifications of life,
see Rudolph Makkreel, Dilthey. Philosopher of the Human Studies
(Princeton: Princeton University Press, 1975), pp. 306-307.

[15] Bernard Lonergan, Collection, ed. F. E. Crowe (New York:
Herder and Herder, 1967), p. 222.

[16] Ibid., p. 223.

[17] On the notion of consciousness, see Section 5 below.

[18] Outstanding employments of the notion of horizon are those
of Kant and Husserl. For Kant "the horizon thus concerns judgment
on, and determination of, what man can know, what he needs to
know, and what he should know." He employs the notion in his
discussion of the extensive and intensive magnitude of cognition.
This is the notion in its familiar analogous sense. See Kant's
Logic, trans. Robert Hartman and Wolfgang Schwarz (Indianapolis:
Bobbs-Merrill, 1974), pp. 44-45. Husserl also employs the notion
in its typical analogous sense. The horizon is the "co-present
margin" of perception, "a dimly apprehended depth or fringe
of indeterminate reality." See Husserl's Ideas: General Introduction to Pure Phenomenology, trans. W. R. Boyce Gibson (London:
Collier-Macmillan, 1962), Section 24. Lonergan's notion of horizon comes closest in meaning to the notion being employed here.
While Lonergan begins with the analogous notion, according to
which a horizon corresponds to one's concern, he also employs
the notion to mean "the group of operations one has mastered"
and "the range of things the subject is conscious of." See the
unpublished transcription of his Lectures on the Philosophy
of Education, 1959, The Lonergan Centre, Toronto, Lecture 4,
p. 10 and Lecture 8, p. 25; see also his unpublished Lecture
on the Philosophy of History, 1960, The Lonergan Centre, Toronto,
p. 11. Other usages of the notion of horizon by Lonergan may
be found in: Collection, pp. 200 and 213-214; A Second Collection,
eds. William Ryan and Bernard Tyrrell (London: Darton, Longman
& Todd, 1974), pp. 69, 142, 162; his unpublished Introduction
to his doctoral thesis Gratia Operans: A Study of the Speculative
Development in the Writings of St. Thomas Aquinas, ca. 1943,
The Lonergan Centre, Toronto, pp. 17-18; his unpublished Notes
on Existentialism, 1957, Thomas More Inst. typescript, The Lonergan Centre, Toronto, p. 17; his unpublished Dublin Lectures

on Insight, 1961, The Lonergan Centre, Toronto, pp. 41-50 on the spontaneous and theoretic subjects; "Merging Horizons: System, Common Sense, Scholarship," Cultural Hermeneutics 1 (1973), 89, 93; his unpublished paper "Method: Trend and Variations," 1974, The Lonergan Centre, Toronto, pp. 5-9; "Aquinas Today: Tradition and Innovation," The Journal of Religion 55, no. 2 (1975), 166-174; "Theology and Praxis," Address to the Catholic Theological Society of America, 1977, The Lonergan Centre, Toronto, p. 14n.42.

[19] The neutrality of these terms cannot be over-emphasized. In our present situation the classicist notion of culture still has currency. The evaluative connotations of 'ordinary' and 'extraordinary', when these words are used in connection with human endeavors, partly derive from this classicist notion. The reader is asked to suspend the classicist notion in the interest of grasping a new model. Our democratic ideals may also have some bearing upon the evaluative employment of these words. In a culture informed by individualistic motives, no one desires to be "merely ordinary". In contrast, the use of 'ordinary' in the present essay is akin to its use by analysts of ordinary language.

[20] For Aristotle, every aisthesis is an aisthesis aistheseos. See De Anima 425b12 ff. and Metaphysics 12.9. See also H.-G. Gadamer, Philosophical Hermeneutics, trans. and ed. David E. Linge (Berkeley: University of California Press, 1976), p. 123. For Descartes, a thought is not only consciousness of its object, but always at the same time consciousness of itself. See Pierre Thevenaz, What is Phenomenology?, ed. James M. Edie (Chicago: Quadrangle Books, 1962), p. 165. For Brentano, in every psychic phenomenon there is always consciousness of self besides the primarily intended object. See Thevenaz, p. 105. For Sartre, all positional consciousness of objects is accompanied by a non-positional consciousness of self. See Thevenaz, p. 105, and J.-P. Sartre, The Transcendence of the Ego, trans. Williams and Kirkpatrick (New York: The Noonday Press, 1957), pp. 40-41. A Scholastic structural distinction between actus signatus and actus exercitus points in the same direction: "I am saying I see something" differs from "I see something", but the signification is not the initial awareness of the act of seeing; the exercise of the act of seeing is something in which my own operation is present to me. See Lonergan, A Second Collection, p. 150; his unpublished Notes on Mathematical Logic, 1957, The Lonergan Centre, Toronto, 1.3. See also, H.-G. Gadamer, Philosophical Hermeneutics, p. 123, where Heidegger's rediscovery of this distinction is recalled.

[21] Scientific performance has been investigated at length by Lonergan in Insight: A Study of Human Understanding (New York: Philosophical Library, 1958), Part I.

[22] Lonergan has thoroughly worked out the implications of this important distinction between experience and knowledge. It is fundamental throughout his works. See, for example, Insight, p. 672 on the distinction between experience and verification through grasp of the unconditioned in judgment, and Collection, pp. 226-227 on experience, self-presence, and self-knowledge. A distinction between the experience of oneself and knowledge of oneself is also made in ordinary language. The initial movement away from mere self-experience in the direction of explicit self-knowledge is signaled occasionally in interpersonal conversation by the introductory phrase, "Now that you mention it ...". For example, if I am told by another that I seem to have a bad conscience, I may respond, "Now that you mention it, I do." This initial movement is normally accompanied by typical affective correlates of discovery, such as temporary exhilaration and release of frustration. For a psychological discussion of the act of insight generally as augmenting mere experience, see Eliot D. Hutchinson, How to Think Creatively (New York: Abingdon Press, 1949).

[23] See Lonergan, Insight, p. 375 on the notion of a mentality.

[24] Ibid., pp. 705-706 on the symbiosis of knowledge and belief, and the group mentality.

[25] The four-act structure -- experiencing, understanding, judgment, and decision -- and its affective context or medium are central topics of Lonergan's Insight and Method in Theology. For compendious accounts of the incremental process of coming-to-know, see Method in Theology, Chap. 1 and Collection, pp. 221-239. On the full range of cognitional activities involved in the scientific construction and verification of a systematic scientific synthesis, see Insight, Chaps. I-IV.

[26] Lonergan, Insight, Chap. XI; Method in Theology, Chap. I. The second name is later than the first; it differs in that activities of evaluation, deliberation and decision are explicitly included in its reference. See John Henry Newman, A Grammar of Assent (New York: Image Books, 1955), pp. 396-397, and Johannes Artz, "Newman as Philosopher," International Philosophical Quarterly 16 (1976), 263-297, especially p. 268. See also, Newman's The Idea of a University (New York: Image Books, 1959), pp. 129-130 on the "master view of things". See, finally, Karl-Otto Apel, Towards a Transformation of Philosophy, trans. Glyn Adey and David Frisby (London; Boston: Routledge & Kegan Paul, 1980), p. 46.

[27] See, for example, Michael D. Biddis, The Age of the Masses (Harmondsworth: Penguin, 1977).

[28] On the spontaneous nature of commonsense operation, see

Lonergan, _Insight_, pp. 173–176. See also, Alfred Schutz and Thomas Luckmann, _The Structures of the Life-World_, trans. Richard M. Zaner and H. Tristram Engelhardt, Jr. (Evanston: Northwestern University Press, 1973), p. 27; Edmund Husserl, _Ideas_, Section 27, and _The Crisis of European Sciences and Transcendental Phenomenology_, trans. David Carr (Evanston: Northwestern University Press, 1970), Part IIIA, Section 38.

[30]On the ordinary mode of operation as habitual, see Lonergan, _Insight_, pp. 175–176; Schutz and Luckmann, _The Structures of the Life-World_, Chap. 3. Lonergan speaks of the "habitual nucleus of insights" while Schutz and Luckmann speak of the "sedimentation of the stock of knowledge". A contrasting view, emphasizing "principles of common sense", rather than operations, is offered by H. H. Price, "The Appeal to Common Sense," _Philosophy_ 5 (1930), 24–35, 191–202.

[31]The word is used here in its classicist sense.

[32] A fairly systematic account of the variety of depths or levels on which a 'classic', for example, may be read is offered by Mortimer Adler, _How To Read A Book_ (New York: Simon and Schuster, 1940), pp. 266–268. It is interesting to note that Adler's three groups of rules for reading correspond to the three initial sets of acts in the sequence of sets constitutive of the deep mode of operation on Lonergan's account: experience, understanding, judging. More relevant in the present connection is Adler's distinction between reading within one's horizon and reading that leads one beyond one's horizon. See pp. 31–32.

[33] H. H. Price has made a similar point with reference to philosophic subjects in "The Appeal to Common Sense," pp. 25–26: "However sophisticated we may be with the study of philosophy—however much afflicted with what Reid calls 'metaphysical lunacy'—we can always appeal, as it were, to the plain man within our own heart. We can slip back without difficulty into the common-sense state of mind, and, of course, we constantly do so, even against our will. When we are in that state of mind we make the same judgments as any ordinary non-philosophical person would make if he were in our place; we claim to apprehend the same sort of facts and the same sort of things and relations as he does." As we shall see in Chapter II, Section 2, the 'slipping back' of the philosopher in particular, when he is seking to integrate in thought the full range of horizons, may result in the obfuscation of relevant data. See also Lonergan's account of philosophic activity in a problematic relation to the preserved commonsense starting-point, in _Insight_, pp. 416–421.

[34] Of these notions the least familiar is perhaps the notion of a scholarly horizon. The notion does seem appropriate as a designation in the final list for that horizon which has set

30

itself apart from the others at least since Cicero articulated his oratorical/literary ideal.

[35] See, for example, R. G. Collingwood, Speculum Mentis, or the Map of Knowledge (Oxford: Clarendon Press, 1924, 1970), p. 42; see also Lonergan, Method in Theology, the Index under "differentiations of consciousness"; see also Peter Winch, The Idea of a Social Science and its Relation to Philosophy (London: Routledge & Kegan Paul, 1963), p. 41, 100-101.

[36] See Ernst Cassirer, The Philosophy of Symbolic Forms, trans. Ralph Mannheim (New Haven, London: Yale University Press, 1957), Vol. III, pp. 205-277; Bruno Snell, The Discovery of the Mind (New York: Harper Torchbooks, 1960), Chaps. 1, 3, 5 and 9.

[37] Those familiar with Lonergan's treatment of differentiations of consciousness and realms of meaning will note the similarity between my account of combinations and his account of differentiations. See his Method in Theology, pp. 275-276. Lonergan's differentiations correspond to modes of operation as extraordinary, and his notion of undifferentiated consciousness corresponds to the ordinary mode of operation.

II

THE HEURISTIC SIGNIFICANCE OF THE MODEL

Before turning, in Chapter III, to the dynamic aspect of groups of horizons, the model at this basic stage of its development may be compared and contrasted with other more familiar models. The purpose of this comparison and contrast is to promote further understanding of the horizonal structure and its heuristic significance. First, the horizonal structure will be distinguished from a range of familiar sociological schemes. Secondly, it will be distinguished from two familiar philosophic shemes. My discussion of sociological categories is meant to bring to light the need for a recognition of horiznal differences by students of internal cultural relations. Besides sociological and economic variables, there are horizonal variables which should be taken into account when contentious and non-contentious human relations are studied. My subsequent discussion of two philosophic schemes is meant to underscore the fact that the horizonal structure is one model which is relatively free of the kinds of commitments that predetermine the outcomes of investigations.

1. SOCIOLOGICAL CATEGORIES

By employing distinctions between castes, estates, classes, professions, and elites sociologists may account for a wide variety of types of contentious and non-contentious human relationships. But the horizonal differences recorded in common linguistic usage are also relevant to the study of internal cultural relations. To some extent, imperfect and imprecise understanding of horizonal differences plays a role in that spontaneous process of sizing-up others and ourselves by which we situate ourselves socially and by which we account for contentious and non-contentious interpersonal events. "He's an intellectual, lacking in all practicality," we may say. "No wonder he can't get the point." Again, "He is a practical man like myself. We understand each other." More often than not, imprecise appeals to horizonal differences are expressed evaluatively, as are appeals to socio-economic differences. These self-situating accounts may be generated partially by advertence to socio-economic status; but, once ascertained, socio-economic status may serve only to confirm a suspicion of horizonal difference. In what are commonly named class conflict, caste conflict, estate conflict, conflict between professions, and conflicts of elites there may be an element of horizonal conflict; and in what are commonly thought to be purely socio-economic instances of cooperation, there may be an element of horizonal conciliation. If students of culture are alerted to the possible influence of horizonal differences on human relationships and cultural stability, their accounts of the formation, reproduction, and deformation of culture may be rendered more concretely adequate. While the conception of a culture as a dynamic structure of horizons does not imply that the horizonal variable is the most fundamental variable to be studied in any particular case of conflict or harmony, it does imply that the horizonal variable will be heuristically significant in some cases.

1.1. HORIZONS AND CASTES

Horizons are to be distinguished from castes. A caste is a hereditary, endogamous, occupational group whose position in a hierarchy is fixed by what sociologists have named a ritual distance. The purest example of a caste system was the Hindu system of India. In theory at least, Hindus belonged to one of four main groups. In order of precedence they were the warrior group, the priestly group, the trading and manufacturing group, and the servants and slaves.[1]

Is the priestly group identical with the religious horizon? If a man were a servant or slave, he could not be a priest; if he were a merchant, he could not be a warrior. The possibilities of combination of horizons in a single subject have already been outlined. It is evident that a single subject may be both a philosopher and an artist, a scholar and a religious man, a philosopher and a religious man, an ordinary subject and a religious one. Accord-

34

ingly, it was not only the priestly caste that was religious; for the warriors, the merchants, the artisans, and the slaves were all Hindus in name, and some in each group may be assumed to have been religious in fact. The priestly group is not identical with the religious horizon. Caste divisions are more specific than horizonal divisions. Horizonal divisions are grounded upon an advertence to the internal data of modes of operation and standpoints rather than upon the external data of social role and economic status.

1.2. HORIZONS AND ESTATES

Horizons are to be distinguished from estates. An estate is not a position in the ritual order but a social and legal position determined by man-made, but supposedly divinely-inspired, laws of social life. In Sweden, for example, until the latter part of the nineteenth century, Nobles, Clergy, Citizens, and Peasants were distinguished by their respective legal rights and duties.[2] But there were religious Citizens, Nobles, and Peasants, and perhaps there were irreligious Clergy. In Denmark, certainly, there were Clergy who felt the sting of Kierkegaard's attack upon Christendom. Again, among the Clergy, Citizens, and Peasants one might have found scholars, mystics, artists, and philosophers. All ordinary subjects were not Peasants. Moreover, a king might at any time ennoble a distinguished servant, or grant legal immunity from the normal operation of feudal laws to whole cities. But the servant did not become at that moment a philosopher or a scientist, and a city's inhabitants did not instantly become polymaths. A king cannot make a philosopher of an ordinary man, or a mystic of a scientist. At most, he can provide the material means prerequisite to a personal task of intellectual and affective development. One may think, for example, of the central place held by the discussion of economic matters in the letters to Dionysius commonly attributed to Plato. In one of these letters, too, the view is expressed that it is a natural law that wisdom and great power attract each other.[3] However, wisdom and great power are seldom possessed by a single man or woman. The great power of a king is his authority over the affairs of everyday life with which everyone must deal either intermittently or continuously. His rule may be guided by the dictates of a philosophic horizon, the higher perspective of a mystical horizon, the

35

sensitivity and imagination of an artistic horizon. But, for the most part, the ordinary horizon is the horizon of kings as such.[4] Estate divisions are not horizonal divisions; they do not have the same generality.

1.3. HORIZONS AND CLASSES

Horizons are to be distinguished from classes. Marx argued that classes are to be defined in terms of their relationship to the instruments of production and the distribution of wealth.[5] Classes have an economic basis. But, as Edmond Goblot has noted, intellectuals (extraordinary subjects considered as a set) do not constitute special classes and still less one class.[6] Intellectuals may be bourgeois; but, if they are bourgeois only because of their intellectual mode of operation, they are of comparatively low rank. Further, while it is perhaps true that, for the bourgeois, intellectual work is deemed more honorable than the work of the body or manual labor, it is thought to be even more honorable not to work at all and to live on one's income.[7] Intellectual work is preferred because it has a less deteriorating effect on the body, and not because of its intrinsic worth. It is preferred for the ultimately practical reason that it promotes indirectly the prolongation of life. On the other hand, for the intellectual as such, living on one's income is neither honorable nor dishonorable; it is valued inasmuch as it liberates him for extraordinary endeavors, eliminating the need to return frequently and for long periods of time to the ordinary starting-point.

As the set of extraordinary horizons is not what is meant by the bourgeoisie, so the ordinary horizon is not what is meant by the proletariat. This distinction is especially important, for it is the one most easily overlooked by Marxian and other contemporary thinkers. In its Marxian sense, the proletariat is the class of rural and urban industrial workers who must work to live because they own no capital; they have only their own labor.[8] As ownership of the means of production does not strictly imply an artistic, scientific, scholarly, philosophic, or mystical standpoint, world, and mode of operation, so manual labor does not strictly imply an ordinary standpoint, world, and mode.[9] Eric Hoffer, for example, was both a longshoreman and a philosopher of life, and Spinoza was a lens grinder.[10]

The familiar notions of class consciousness and class conflict are not essential to an understanding of the relationship of a single horizon to itself or of many horizons to one another. The growing awareness by the proletariat of its class position vis à vis the bourgeoisie is not the same as the growing awareness by the ordinary subject of his horizonal position vis à vis the set of extraordinary horizons.[11] Class consciousness may in fact block the emergence of horizonal consciousness, for its emergence presupposes a dominance of thinking by the category of class. On the other hand, horizonal consciousness may mitigate the socially disruptive consequences of emerging class consciousness without blocking needed transformations; for its emergence implies a familiarity with a larger range of variables relevant to the understanding of human conflict in general. By itself class consciousness escalates class conflict, the process of gradual approximation to an economically just utopia.[12] On the other hand, if horizonal differences do partially ground many interpersonal conflicts, then horizonal consciousness is a necessary condition for the possibility of harmony in some human endeavors.

However, the notion of class consciousness is also employed in a loose and general way to signify a group's self-awareness through the members sharing a common consumption pattern.[13] The self-consciousness of horizons is analogous to this more general notion. The key terms, though, must be changed. By self-awareness and self-consciousness one must understand not mere self-presence but some degree of self-understanding and self-knowledge. For "consumption pattern" one must substitute "standpoint, world, and mode of operation". For 'class' one must substitute 'horizon'. The self-understanding of a horizon emerges in part through the subjects sharing a common world, standpoint, and mode of operation. Ordinary subjects seek the company of other ordinary subjects, artists congregate in particular districts and localities, philosophers gather for conferences, and this gathering-together to share expressions of aims, procedures, techniques, and so on promotes the understanding by sets of subjects of their respective horizons.[14]

In Marxian theory the significant class conflict is the mortal conflict between the bourgeoisie and the proletariat, and it has its roots in conflicting interests arising from different relations to the means of production. Class conflict is escalated by the emergence of class consciousness. Horizonal conflict, on the other hand, has its roots in distinct relations of distinct standpoints to distinct worlds which are more or less adequate approximations to the universe of being.[15] The horizonal conflict that stands forth at the present time, I believe, is that between the ordinary horizon and the set of extraordinary horizons. But this horizonal conflict is not necessarily escalated by the emergence of a degree of self-knowledge. For every extraordinary subject, although beyond the horizon of the ordinary subject, is always capable of empathizing with the ordinary subject. Every extraordinary horizon emerges out of an original ordinary horizon; ordinary self-presence is preserved in extraordinary self-presence. The horizonal self-knowledge of an extraordinary subject, if achieved with thoroughness, would include ordinary self-knowledge. On the other hand, not every bourgeois was first a proletarian. Consequently, the emergence of both bourgeois and proletarian class consciousness most often results in an increase in interpersonal and group tensions that can find their release only in class war. Conflict analysis, which emphasizes the notion of class conflict alone, seems destined from the start to conclude that interpersonal and group tensions can find their reduction and release only in violent confrontation. A preoccupation with the category of class in conflict analysis serves to remove any hope one may have had of promoting mutual comprehension, and so also of avoiding violent confrontation, by exploiting empathic ability. If horizonal conflict is partially constitutive of human disharmony, then, analysis of social conflict strictly in terms of class conflict is excessively abstract analysis. Without an explicit notion of horizonal conflict, elements of social conflict having their roots in horizonal differences will be discounted or completely overlooked. The reduction, in Marxian theory, of extraordinary expression to privilege-preserving ideology is an example of the abstractness of conflict analysis which overlooks horizonal differences. Abstract conflict analysis bows before the concrete, lapsing into performative if not logical incoherence. Marx's own expression was extraordinary, and yet Marx maintained an intention of absoluteness or objectivity in his expression. Consequently, there arises for Marxian theorists a troubling problem: Can extraordinary expression be both objective and ideological? Even the extraordinary assumption of the primacy of the ordinary standpoint, world, and mode of operation, which underpins the conclusion that intellectuals shun labor for ultimately <u>practical reasons</u>, falls into the category of privilege-preserving ideology. If horizonal differences do in fact play a role in some conflicts, then the notion of class conflict is an inadequate tool for the dissection of those conflicts. Class conflict does not normally occur in complete isolation from factual horizonal relationships; and horizonal conflict can occur where class conflict is absent. The notion of horizon, then, introduces into the analysis of human conflicts another variable which, if taken fully into account, may render conflict analysis more concretely adequate.

1.4. HORIZONS AND PROFESSIONS

A profession is an occupation or vocation requiring training in the liberal arts and/or the sciences and advanced study in a specialized field.[16] Criteria for determining professional status are time spent in classrooms, passing grades on examinations, and use of acquired credentials to gain a livelihood. Extraordinary horizons stand to professions as horizons in general stand to classes. One may be a scientist without having met these criteria. A scientist may or may not be a professional, that is, one engaged in scientific activity as a source of livelihood. On the other hand, a professional scientist may or may not be operating from a properly scientific standpoint. This may be illustrated by considering the Aristotelian notion of science. For Aristotle, science was certain knowledge of things through their causes. But one may attempt to do science strictly in terms of the ten predicaments, without adverting to causes. Again, modern science pins its faith on its method; but there are professional scientists who are unable to construct a properly controlled experimental situation. Finally, the differences between extraordinary horizons and professions may be easily exhibited by appealing to ordinary experience. One may think, for example, of the otherworldly mystic who seeks no employment whatever, and of the unemployed by still active scholar or philosopher.

1.5. HORIZONS AND ELITES

In his Notes Towards a Definition of Culture T. S. Eliot distinguished between classes and elites. Elites are approximately the horizons which I have distinguished, but there remains a subtle difference which has its roots once again in an emphasis of the sociological point of view.

Classes, it is commonly supposed, could disappear; but elites will remain. For elites are groups of superior individuals, and qualitative differences between individuals exist within classes, and they will exist without them.

It seems to me that at the stage of the sharpest division into classes we can distinguish an elite also. Are we to believe that the artists of the Middle Ages were all men of noble rank, or that the hierarchy and the statesmen were all selected according to their pedigree?[17]

The qualities in virtue of which the original members of the elite attained their position were not all transmitted equally to their descendants.[18] Discussion of elites involves a good deal more than government and the governing class, says Eliot.[19] The dominant tendency, however, has been to focus attention upon the ruling classes, rather than upon elites.

Culture, according to Eliot, means the several kinds of attainment of elites taken together.[20] This notion of culture is similar to my notion of culture as a dynamic structure of horizons. Eliot distinguishes (i) governmental or political elites, (ii) administrative or organizing elites, (iii) artistic elites, (iv) scientific elites, (v) philosophic elites, (vi) moral-religious elites or groups consisting of men of action.[21] According to their social functions, he distinguishes governmental/political elites, on the one hand, from artistic, scientific, philosophic, and moral-religious elites on the other.[22] The former expedite the daily struggle for existence, while the latter sublimate psychic energies not fully exhausted by that struggle.

The political and organizing elites expedite the daily struggle for existence by persuading and coordinating human wills. They are groups of leaders.[23] Within the horizonal structure, the ordinary horizon includes the highly developed practical and dramatic

40

mode of operation of politicians and administrators, but it also includes the practical and dramatic mode of operation of the followers who simply earn a living and run their own lives. Social function is more fundamental in Eliot's classification of elites than mode of operation. Eliot's sublimating elite corresponds to the set of extraordinary horizons, but the correspondence is not an identity. Extraordinary horizons are most easily identified by adverting to group formations of extraordinary individuals. But extraordinary horizons are not groups. Horizonal development influences group formation to some degree in almost every significant case. Elites stand to horizons as groups of obviously extraordinary individuals sharing a common concern stand to the shared standpoint, mode of operation, and worlds of those individuals who constitute the groups. While Eliot is careful to distinguish himself from K. Mannheim, who emphasized classes even more strongly, he does not move completely beyond the sociological point of view.[24]

The dominance of the sociological point of view in Eliot's theory of elites is reflected by his concern with the problem of the isolation of elites from one another. Eliot appreciates the need for some degree of departmentalization of elites; but he feels that the increasing isolation of elites from one another inhibits the circulation of ideas and the flow of intersubjective influence. There arises the problem of formation, preservation and development of elites or superior groups of individuals. But the prior question, one more significant for an understanding of the relations of elites to one another, regards the formation, preservation, and development of distinct horizons. The problem of the fragmentation of elites, while not completely separable from the problem of social formation, is also related to the philosophic problem of the identity of worlds, standpoints, and modes of operation. Had Eliot noted adequately the relevance of horizonal formation to the formation of distinct elites, he might not have permitted a sociological emphasis of groups to force upon him a distinction between the governmental/administrative groups and men of common sense in general. The man of common sense is practical and dramatic, and the function of a persuasive and coordinating group of men of common sense does not presuppose a shift in basic horizon but only a difference in social position. Eliot adverted only to obviously socially significant

41

groups, perhaps because he maintained too narrow a notion of culture, one which excludes all but superior individuals.

Horizons are not castes, estates, classes, professions, or elites, although these are related to horizons as social and economic status and social role are related to horizonal development. Social and economic status constitute material conditions of horizonal development, and in this respect they reflect horizonal differentiation covertly and inadequately. The distinction between a priestly caste and a servant caste reflects social role differentiation directly; but it also covertly reflects the broader horizonal distinction between the religious subject and the ordinary subject. The distinction between the proletariat and the bourgeoisie reflects social role differentiation and economic status directly; but it indirectly reflects the horizonal distinction between the ordinary horizon and the set of extraordinary horizons. However, distinctions based in social and economic status are inadequate tools for the task of understanding the causes of human disharmony in many situations in which it emerges. They bring a certain range of causes to light, but another range of causes is left in the shadows. As these distinctions are inadequate for the dissection of human disharmony in many cases, so they are insufficient for the task of understanding human relations in general.

Besides covertly and inadequately reflecting horizonal differentiation, socio-economic status partially determines horizonal development. A Hindu servant may reach a high level of religious development, but he probably will never become a scholar. A proletarian may have highly developed native intelligence, but he probably will never become a scholar or a scientist. While I do not think socio-economic status should be ignored by students of culture, for just this reason, I do think its significance is in need of careful qualification, especially in our day when Marxian theory has acquired so many adherents. Marxian theory, I have suggested, is involved in an ultimate incoherence despite its limited relevance to conflict analysis.[25] Opportunity is often a function of social status, and horizonal development is dependent upon the emergence of opportunities. But opportunity is not only a function of social status. It is also a function, in our day, of random

42

social constellations prepared by travel and electronic communication.

The general conclusion to be drawn from this comparison and contrast is that the horizonal structure cuts across the boundaries that separate castes, estates, classes, professions and elites. It directs the student of cultural matrices to additional variables which he may otherwise overlook in his investigations of cultural relations. But it is not to be assumed that horizonal differences are more basic or more fundamental than social and economic differences for the study of human relations. Horizonal difference is not the ultimate root of human conflict, nor is it the only notion to be employed in the study of human relations. Moreover, besides social and economic bases, human conflicts also have psychological roots. By introducing the notion of horizonal difference, I have introduced another variable to be taken into account in the study of man; it does not displace but rather supplements the social, economic, and psychological variables already employed as heuristic devices.

2. PHILOSOPHIC COMMITMENTS

The basic elements of the horizonal structure have been exposed. In Chapter III the model will be determined further by a treatment of the dynamic aspect of cultural matrices. So far the following terms have been employed for the construction of the model: culture; structure; horizon; ordinary and extraordinary; experience and knowledge; standpoint, mode of operation, world; expression; combination. Identification of the distinct horizons and their number has been facilitated by an additional six terms: ordinary horizon; artistic horizon; scientific horizon; philosophic horizon; scholarly horizon; religious horizon. Words and phrases have been found in ordinary and extraordinary linguistic expression which point to ordinary and extraordinary worlds, standpoints, and modes of operation. Ambiguities in ordinary and extraordinary expression have been accounted for by means of a distinction between consciousness and self-knowledge and a brief reflection upon the specific limitations of the ordinary horizon. Every horizon is a function of subjective development,[26] and every extraordinary horizon is beyond the ordinary horizon. This emerging model has been compared with less general sociological structures

43

to which investigators may be inclined to appeal when they turn to a consideration of cultures, and its heuristic significance for the study of internal cultural relations has been noted. I propose now to illustrate further the value of the structure as a model by directing attention to its philosophic presuppositions.

2.1. THE PROBLEM OF OBJECTIVITY

One principle operation in the formulation of the model has already been mentioned and employed. Distinct worlds strictly imply distinct standpoints and modes of operation. This principle grounds the unity of a horizon; but it also provides the grounds for a serious problem of objectivity. However, to affirm that a subject's world is at the very least a world-for-a-subject is not to commit oneself to an idealism, even though it raises the specter of idealism. Fear of idealist implications may lead a thinker to affirm inadvertently the existence of idealist implications. But this is an illogical transition, it prejudges the issue, and it is to be a-voided. It is certainly incumbent upon philosophers to explain how it is that a multiplicity of worlds-for-subjects can be related to a single universe of being. But the existence of this philosophic problem does not alter the facts which give rise to the problem in the first instance, viz., the actual existence of a multiplicity of worlds-for-subjects and the actual maintenance of an intention of objectivity by all of these subjects whose worlds differ.[27] Newman remarked that ten thousand difficulties do not make a doubt, and the point is well-taken. Difficulties pertain to the personal task of solving a problem, but doubt pertains to the facts which give rise to the problem.[28]

Neither a subjectivist nor an objectivist standpoint is presupposed by the horizonal structure. Both objectivism and subjectivism pertain to the question of the absolute objectivity of knowledge. Objectivists maintain that the object is decisive for the objectivity of knowledge. Subjectivists maintain that the dispositions and states of the subject are decisive. Objectivism implies the denial of the actual existence of a multiplicity of worlds-for-subjects; it conceives subjectivity as "mere subjectivity", the interference of arbitrary and capricious dispositions and states with the context-free appre-

44

hension of just what is there. Subjectivism implies the denial of the fact that subjects have an intention of objectivity, and it leads eventually to radical relativism. Objectivism implies a disregard of the subject, his standpoint, and his operations, while subjectivism eliminates the heuristic notion of a single universe of being. The horizonal structure, on the other hand, presupposes the actual existence of a multiplicity of worlds-for-subjects and the actual maintenance of an intention of objectivity by all of these subjects whose worlds differ, but it does not presuppose a specific stand on the grounds of absolutely objective knowledge.[29]

Underlying the horizonal structure is an anticipation of a middle ground, a third way which leads neither to radical relativism and an abandonment of the intention of objectivity nor to radical objectivism and a denial of the significance of subjectivity. The horizonal structure is simply a model, a formula for finding, a guide for inquiry, to be employed for the purpose of exposing the features of a given cultural matrix. Within the boundaries that have been drawn, the problem of the objectivity of the knowledge acquired or implemented by any of the six horizons does not need to be addressed. In fact, claims of greater objectivity and accusations of mere subjectivity are themselves expressions of philosophic commitments which are constitutive of horizonal relations in a given milieu. Horizonal relations are strained by expressions of conflicting philosophic commitments. The purpose of formulating the model is to expose general features of cultural matrices and not to institute or to participate in horizonal conflicts. Accordingly, where the term 'object' is employed, it is used in the same way as 'world'. By 'object' is not meant an object of sense, as an ordinary subject might assume, for then I would be begging the question of horizonal superiority. More generally, 'object' does not mean "that which stands opposite" (Gegenstand, objet, oggetto, obiectum, to antikeimenon), for this meaning is an expression of the biologically-based, extroverted relation of subject to object, and it is not specifically cognitional; its use implies that the relation between subject and object is not constituted by subjective operations in the first instance.[30] Rather, the term is to be employed in the very broad sense of "object of a mode of operation" or "object of a subject". Similarly, 'subject' does not mean "subject of activities of sensing or perceiving" but "subject of

45

a mode of operation". Sensing and perceiving are not the sole constituents of modes of operation.[31]

2.2. CONSCIOUSNESS AND SELF-KNOWLEDGE

A distinction has also been drawn between self-presence and self-knowledge which parallels the distinction implemented by scientists between physical seeing, in the popular sense, and scientific observation, description, explanation, and judgment. This distinction generates philosophic questions regarding the nature of consciousness, the possibility and fruitfulness of introspection, the danger of infinite regression of conscious acts, and so on. But my employment of the distinction does not entail a commitment regarding any of these philosophic issues.

Common or general usage suggests that a subject's mode of operation may be part of his world. The mode is at least an experienced part of his world, if not an understood and known part. Linguistic evidence renders legitimate the use of a generalized notion of experience that may be employed to refer to data of sense and to data of consciousness. As a matter of fact, designations for modes of operation are employed by ordinary and extraordinary subjects. We do not find designations for worlds alone, without any mention of modes of operation and standpoints. It follows that ordinary and extraordinary subjects presume themselves to have access, by whatever means, to data other than sensible data upon which they may base their understanding of themselves and their contemporaries. Differences in degree of specificity, discernible in ordinary and extraordinary designations of modes, imply different degrees of exploitation of this access. To accommodate the existence of the designations and the differences in their degree of specificity, the notions of self-presence as such and conscious data as understood and known were introduced. Philosophic reflection must 'save' these phenomena and so preserve and refine the distinction employed to accommodate them. Philosophers may escape this task only by assuming that ordinary and extraordinary subjects are self-deceived, but this assumption is radically self-defeating. The only philosophic commitment implied by the use of the distinction is a commitment to the preservation of common linguistic usage.

46

2.3. NEGATIVE COMMITMENTS

The commitments implicit in the model are not positive as much as they are negative. There is a commitment to the exclusion of evaluative terminology in the formulation of the horizonal structure. This commitment must be made if one is to avoid an arbitrary limitation of the range of possible horizonal relationships. For example, if the evaluative designations of the ordinary horizon, common in extraordinary expression, were employed to designate the ordinary horizon, the horizonal structure would become a reflection of horizonal relations at the present time rather than remaining an open framework for the study of relations in any period. Again, if the evaluative designations of extraordinary horizons, common in Marxian theory, were employed, a similar difficulty would arise.

There is also a commitment to parsimony in epistemological and ontological matters. The horizonal structure must permit the investigator to take the range of human endeavors as he finds them, without determining beforehand the ontological status of their worlds or the objectivity of their modes of operation, and each is to be given equal weight as a possibly objective and worthwhile human endeavor.

These two negative commitments are coincident with the ends for which the model is to be employed. It is a heuristic structure, and it is to be employed to _expose_ and not to _predetermine_, _justify_, _rationalize_, or _preserve privilege_. The degree and extent of philosophic commitment involved in the employment of the model may be illustrated by contrasting the horizonal structure, first, with Aristotle's scheme of ways of life and, second, with William James' scheme of sub-worlds.

2.4. WAYS OF LIFE

Even today, when we distinguish theoreticians from practical men, we usually have in mind Aristotle's distinction between _theoria_ and _praxis_. This distinction is both current and laden with question-begging presuppositions.

Aristotle reserved the notion of ways of life for those lives chosen in freedom, in independence from the necessities of life and the relationships

47

they originate. There were three ways of life: the
life of enjoyment of bodily pleasures, the life of
the philosopher, and the political life.[32] The lives
of slaves, free craftsmen, and merchants were less
dignified than the aesthetic, philosophic and political lives. The polis-life was the properly human
life; the philosophic life was an 'immortalizing'
life, seeking what is above man; the lives of slaves,
free craftsmen, and merchants were subhuman.[33] The
Aristotelian distinction between theoria and praxis
was basically a distinction between walks of life;
it was not a distinction between thinking and acting,
thinking about life and living life. Aristotle employed 'praxis' in several ways. In the most technical
sense, praxis was man's free activity in the realm
of political life. In a less determinate sense, praxis
included making, which has its end outside itself,
and even seeing, thinking and intellection.[35] For
the most part, however, praxis pertained to the bios
politikos and the realm of human affairs. Theoria,
on the other hand, pertained to the philosophic life
concerned with three objects of contemplation --
the universal and imperishable features of nature,
the mathematical realm, and first causes.[36]

As Hannah Arendt has noted, Aristotle's very
articulation of the different ways of life was guided
by the ideal of theoria; the decisive distinction
is not that between theoria and praxis, philosophic
life and polis-life, but a distinction between quiet
(scholē) and unquiet (ascholia).[37] This passage from
Aristotle's Politics plainly reveals Aristotle's
preference for the absolute quiet of theoria.

> The preference which we give to the parts of life
> and their different activities will inevitably
> follow the same general line as those which we
> give to the parts of the soul and their different
> activities. War must therefore be regarded as
> only a means to peace; action as a means to leisure;
> and acts which are merely necessary, or merely
> and simply useful, as means to acts which are
> good in themselves.[38]

The Greek preference for absolute rest in contemplation was taken to its limit in the medieval formulation of the distinction between the vita activa
and the vita contemplativa. Praxis came to be considered one of the necessities of earthly life as well,
and the bios theoretikos (vita contemplativa) stood
alone as the only truly free way of life.[39]

48

To complete this sketch of the Aristotelian scheme, a scheme which has had enormous influence upon characterizations of cultural relations,[40] it should be noted that the Greeks of the fourth and third centuries B.C. did not share our contemporary notion of the unity of mankind. Consequently, the arrangement of ways of life is also an arrangement of levels of manhood. Aristotle distinguished men from animals because man alone of all animals stands erect and has hands which serve as universal tools. But a further distinction was made between men who are capable of leading a truly human life, those who used the logos, and those who did not use the logos.[41] Logos did not mean "cognitive faculty" or 'rationality' but rather rationality as it expressed itself in speech that was articulate. The actual expression of rationality in articulate speech was given more weight as a criterion of humanity than was the mere possession of rationality. In the context of this distinction, Aristotle's division of lives into those that are properly human and those that are subhuman is understandable.

2.4.1. HORIZONS AND WAYS OF LIFE

The horizonal structure differs from Aristotle's scheme of ways of life. The horizonal structure is broader, and it does not favor one life in particular. The lives, in the broadest sense, which Aristotle divided into subhuman and human are included in the notion of an ordinary horizon. The ordinary subject may lead the life of a slave, a laborer, a craftsman, a merchant, or a political man without diverging from the ordinary mode of operation.[42] Moreover, the full range of lives -- subhuman, human, and 'immortalizing' -- may be included in the notion of a set of extraordinary horizons. The extraordinary set may include craftsmen who happen to be artists and political men, like the young Plato, who happen to be philosophers. Occupational proximity to the fulfillment of life's basic needs, social or practical, is not an adequate criterion for the determination of a horizon's ordinary or extraordinary status. At best it is only a clue that is inherently inadequate. One may expect a businessman to operate solely in the shrewd manner of ordinary practicality, but he may turn out to be a man like Alfred Schutz who was both a business executive and a preferred student of Edmund Husserl.[43]

The philosophic life is set apart by Aristotle

primarily because it involves a distinct activity that approximates most closely to absolute quietude, and it is preferred to the remaining lives because it is the least dependent of them all. Even the political life requires other men. Inasmuch as the philosophic life involves a different mode of operation, it corresponds to an extraordinary horizon. It is not a _praxis_ either in the technical sense or in the later medieval sense. In the broad sense of _praxis_, however, every horizon is a _praxis_, for every horizon is partially constituted by a cognitive and affective mode of operation. In the technical sense, only the ordinary horizon in one of its possible domains of socio-practical operation -- the political -- is a _praxis_.

Aristotle's division of ways of life was guided by the ideal of _theoria_, but the horizonal structure involves no commitment regarding the relative superiority of horizons. The horizonal structure is neither ancient nor typically modern. While ancient schemes tend to give preference to the contemplative way of life, modern schemes tend to elevate the active life.[44] I have distinguished a variety of human endeavors, but I have not permitted a judgment on the relative proximity of these endeavors to the _scholē_ of contemplation or to the fulfillment of needs to preclude the incorporation of the full range of endeavors into the structure as equally legitimate members of a cultural matrix. I have not permitted the intrusion of a classical ideal of knowledge, as contemplation of eternal things, to determine beforehand my evaluation of the ordinary horizon in a variety of its dimensions. The theoretical mode of operation, standpoint, and world first emerged in Western culture with the Greeks, and this emergence was accompanied by an imperialistic cultural movement. The hierarchical arrangement of ways of life, which entailed the abasement ultimately even of the _vita activa_ to a derivative, secondary position in the Middle Ages, coincided with the emergence of the theoretical mode of operation.[45] The horizonal structure, finally, does not divide members of the taxonomic class, _homo sapiens_, into those that are fully human and those that are subhuman. A man, in accordance with the modern notion of the unity of mankind, is a subject who endeavors, who consciously intends meanings and values, whose life is a conscious and intentional unrest.

2.5. SUB-WORLDS

In his <u>Principles of Psychology</u> William James presents a classificatory scheme which Alfred Schutz combined with Husserl's phenomenological notions in a study of the structures of the life-world. A consideration of James' scheme reveals further the freedom of the horizonal structure from presuppositions which may render the investigation of cultural relations inadequate. The heuristic adequacy of James' scheme is diminished, first, by an unwarranted emphasis of criteria relevant primarily to the operative mode of the ordinary horizon, and, second, by a related objectivism in his approach.

James distinguishes between the universe or total world and various sub-universes or sub-worlds. He makes related distinctions between special men and most men and between the complete philosopher and the popular mind.

> The popular mind conceives of all these sub-worlds more or less disconnectedly; and when dealing with one of them, forgets for the time being its relations to the rest. The complete philosopher is he who seeks not only to assign to every given object of his thought its right place in one or other of these sub-worlds, but he also seeks to determine the relation of each sub-world to the others in the total world which is.[46]

The sub-worlds listed by James are the world of sense, the world of science, the world of ideal relations or abstract truths, the world of common illusions and prejudices, the supernatural world, individual worlds as numerous as men are, the worlds of the insane, and the world of dreams.[47] James affirms that for most men the world of sense is the ultimate or paramount reality.[48]

> For most men, . . . the 'things of sense' hold this prerogative position, and are the absolutely real world's nucleus. Other things, to be sure, may be real for this man or for that--things of science, abstract moral relations, things of the Christian theology, or what not. But even for the special men, these things are usually real with a less real reality than that of the things of sense. They are taken less seriously; and the very utmost that can be said for anyone's belief in them is that it is as strong as his 'belief

in his own senses'.[49]

2.5.1. HORIZONS AND SUB-WORLDS

James' distinction between the universe or total world and various sub-universes or sub-worlds corresponds approximately to the distinction between the universe of being, a heuristic notion, and the six worlds of the horizonal structure. But the sub-worlds of the total world are not the same as the six worlds of the model. In James' scheme, as the first quotation above implies, the popular mind deals with all of the sub-worlds at one time or another, and the complete philosopher seeks to integrate a range of sub-worlds, each of which is properly his own. The popular mind is roughly the ordinary subject. But in the horizonal structure the ordinary subject deals only with his ordinary world, and that world is just one among six. Again, the popular mind differs from the complete philosopher in that it conceives of the sub-worlds, all of which are its own, more or less disconnectedly, while the complete philosopher pursues an understanding of the relations of the various sub-worlds, all of which are his own, to one another. However, in the model, the ordinary subject differs from the philosophic subject in that he has no experience of worlds other than his ordinary world, while the philosophic subject seeks, but does not possess already, experience and synoptic understanding of all other worlds.[50]

If James' sub-worlds are accessible, every one, to the popular mind as such, they cannot be identical with the worlds of the horizonal structure. The six worlds of the model strictly imply six distinct modes of operation and six distinct standpoints. From this difference between sub-worlds and worlds there follows a difference in the conception of that which is to be unified intellectually by the philosopher. The horizonal structure, James' scheme, and all comparable schemes are in fact conceptions of the world of the philosopher seeking a synoptic view of human endeavor. As we shall see, James' scheme suffers from his problematic relation to the ordinary horizon. A distinction between the popular mind as such and the popular mind as that which extraordinary minds have as their original but not permanent standpoint could eliminate this problem in James' scheme.

The last three sub-worlds are excluded from

the horizonal structure. While it is legitimate to speak of individual horizons as numerous as men are, the notion is not very useful to one who aspires to be a complete philosopher. It has some relevance within the philosophic horizon itself to the determination of the various psychological grounds underlying philosophic options in some cases, as both Fichte and James have suggested.[51] However, even if Fichte and James are correct in asserting that realists and idealists, tough-minded and tender-minded, are partially or wholly determined by their temperaments, and this is a further question, philosophic options remain preparatory to the synthetic philosophic task.[52] Again, while it is legitimate to speak of the horizons of the insane or mad, the notion is relevant not to philosophy and the unification of human endeavors in thought but to psychology and the understanding of breakdowns in the ability of subjects to settle upon and pursue a given end. These psychological factors have philosophic implications, but they pertain to the world of psychological investigators primarily. Finally, inasmuch as the dreaming subject is semi-conscious, it is legitimate to speak of a dream-world. But the semi-conscious subject, his world, his images and feelings, are the subject-matter of depth psychology and not properly speaking the subject matter of the student of the full range of human endeavors. Dreaming is not a conscientious or concerted effort; accordingly, the philosopher is not concerned with dreams as such but with the scientific horizon of the psychoanalyst or the neurologist and with the ordinary, artistic, scientific, scholarly, philosophic, or religious horizon of the analysand or patient. James' sub-world of dreams is included in the horizonal structure, but it does not constitute a world.

The world of ideal relations or abstract truths and the world of common illusions or prejudices are problematic. They too belong in the horizonal structure, but they do not constitute worlds in that structure. Contemporary ordinary, scientific, artistic, scholarly, religious, and philosophic subjects all entertain abstract truths and consider ideal relations more or less frequently and grasp their significance more or less adequately. Whatever their horizons, human subjects think abstractly and believe others who have formulated ideal relations. It does not follow, however, that these ideal relations and abstract truths are dealt with in the same way and for the same ends by all subjects. Ideal relations and abstract truths do not constitute a distinct world with a corresponding distinct mode of operation and standpoint.

The world of common illusions and prejudices, idols of the tribe in the Baconian scheme, is common to all men as well, provided they are neither insane nor otherwise incapable of historical existence. Every subject is a historical subject. Men of common sense, artists, scientists, scholars, philosophers, and religious, all are influenced by the idols of their age. This sub-world, then, does not constitute a world in the structure with its own corresponding mode and standpoint. But it is nevertheless included.

The three remaining sub-worlds correspond roughly to worlds in the structure. The world of sense, the world of science, and the supernatural world may be compared with the ordinary, the scientific, and the religious worlds. I have already drawn attention to the difference between James' popular mind and the ordinary subject. The popular mind has experience of all of the sub-worlds and differs from the philosopher only insofar as he fails to pursue an understanding of the relations between them. In the horizonal structure, on the other hand, the ordinary subject is simply ordinary, having experience, in a generalized sense, only of the ordinary world. For James, the scientific subject is basically ordinary, while for us he is an extraordinary subject. The scientific subject not only pursues relational understanding but also has a different apprehension of the universe of being. Scientific experience differs from ordinary experience, just as the scientific mode of operation differs from the ordinary mode. In similar fashion, the philosophic and religious subjects may be distinguished from the ordinary subject.

If only three of the sub-worlds correspond to worlds, the criterion by which James determines sub-worlds must differ from the criterion which generates the worlds of the model. What is James' criterion? I noted that the horizontal structure is neither typically ancient nor typically modern. While ancient schemes tend to favor the contemplative way of life, the modern trend is to favor the active life. Now, for James, the world of sense of most men is the paramount reality. That is to say, for the ordinary subject the ordinary world is the ultimate or paramount reality. Thus far James' position is not problematic. However, he also affirms that the world of practical realities is the paramount reality even for the special man.[53] It is true that the world of sense is taken seriously even by special men or those I have named extraordinary subjects. Most mystics do eat and drink. When scientists walk, they try not to stumble; more significantly, when they enter a laboratory, they are not at a loss to find their way around. The scholarly Johnson's 'refutation' of Berkeley exhibits an extraordinary seriousness about the world of sense. However, James also asserts that special sub-worlds are real to the special man only to the degree that the strength of his belief in their reality approximates to, but does not go beyond, the strength of his "belief in his own senses". This assertion lacks adequate grounds. James affirms that sensible objects are either our realities or the tests of our realities, that conceived objects must show sensible effects or else be disbelieved.[54] This view does reflect modern scientists' views of their own criteria and also the opinions of ordinary subjects regarding their own mode of operation.[55] But is this an adequate expression of scholarly, mystical, philosophic, and artistic criteria? A single example will exhibit the significance of this further question.

Philosophers of human studies do not form a united front on the issues of objectivity in interpretation. There are those who favor what may be broadly termed positivism, and there are those who prefer positions less dominated by current expressions of the method of natural science.[56] The phrase "current expressions of the method of natural science" is employed here intentionally. It is not clear that the method of natural science has been adequately objectified by theorists of natural science.[57] A question, then, remains unanswered, and it is a question that is begged by James' conceptions of belief and reality. Moreover, in ordinary expression 'real' is employed in more than one way. It means sensible or tangible or palpable in one employment, but in others it means genuine as opposed to artificial. James, then, correctly understands at least one of the ordinary meanings of 'real', and he is familiar with the role this meaning plays in expressions of scientific methodology. Are these adequate grounds for the importation of this notion of the real and the related notion of belief into philosophy as tools of complete synthesis? While James states explicitly that reality is a relatedness to our active and emotional life,[58] there is a subtle emphasis of criteria of reality appropriate to the ordinary horizon conceived rather narrowly as subjectivity engaged with sensible objects. This emphasis begs the question of horizonal relations and horizonal legitimacy.[59]

James has inappropriately generalized one ordinary conception of the real and the related notion of belief. In the present context, on the other hand, the meanings of the terms, 'reality' and 'belief', are to be determined by adverting to the variety of horizons from within which apprehensions of the universe of being are sought. James' notion of belief and the related notion of reality pertain only to a descriptive account of the ordinary mode of operation and world. If the ordinary subject as such were capable of providing an account of his mode of operation, he would probably give an account of belief and reality similar to James' account. But the ordinary subject as such does not provide accounts. It is the task of the philosopher to give an account of the ordinary horizon. Moreover, the philosopher is not an ordinary subject, but he also believes. He believes the account he gives of the ordinary mode of operation, for example. This believing is not the believing of which he gives his account. The philosophic world, standpoint, and mode differ from the ordinary world, standpoint, and mode. James remarks that "no mere floating conception, no mere disconnected rarity, ever displaces vivid things or permanent things from our belief. A conception, to prevail, must terminate in the world of orderly sensible experience."[60] It is not immediately clear in what sense a philosophic account of the ordinary mode of operation terminates in the world of sensible experience. A mode of operation is not in the world of sense properly speaking. It is present to the operating subject insofar as the operating subject is conscious. A mode may be known by an operating subject inasmuch as he adverts to, understands, and judges his mode of operation. The judgment does require some type of verification, but it is never simply the type of verification which occurs as a result of reflective attention to sensible consequences. It is verification that occurs as a result of reflective attention to conscious operation, for conscious operations are the data in which an understanding of conscious operation is to be verified. Unlike James' world of sense, the ordinary world includes the ordinary subject as present to himself in his operations. The ordinary mode, rather than

56

being _in_ the world of sense (as something sensible or as something verified in sensible data), is <u>directed towards</u> the world of sense. As such, it is beyond the range of apprehension of James' popular mind, but it is within the apprehensive range of the ordinary subject. The ordinary mode is part of the ordinary world as the ordinary subject is at the very least self-present, but it is not a strictly known or explained part of the ordinary world. It follows, as I have already indicated, that the sensible world of the ordinary horizon is commonly designated inadequately. The use of 'sensible' tends to obscure the non-sensible or conscious component of the ordinary world. In the horizonal structure, the notion of the ordinary world includes the ordinary mode of operation as present to the ordinary subject. Similarly, the notions of extraordinary worlds include the appropriate extraordinary modes as present to, but not necessarily explanatorily known by, the variety of extraordinary subjects.

The philosophic activity of believing the account of ordinary operation, then, sets a limit by its very occurrence to the possibility of generalizing the account of ordinary belief, as though that account were a criterion for the determination of the adequacy of extraordinary horizons. This limit is imposed in two manners. The ordinary account that would probably be offered by an ordinary subject, if he were inclined to attempt an account of his mode of operation, cannot be generalized to apply to extraordinary horizons. Again, the philosophic account of the ordinary mode cannot be generalized to apply to extraordinary horizons. The first account suffers from a deficiency in the ability of the ordinary subject as such to provide an account of his mode of operation. The second account applies <u>only</u> to the ordinary horizon. Both limits have been transgressed in a sense by James. First, the philosopher is not restricted to recording the account of the ordinary mode that any ordinary subject might offer. To be bound by this restriction is to be misled by the occlusive meaning of 'sensible' as that word pertains to the ordinary world. The ordinary world includes the ordinary mode as self-present. Second, the philosopher is not providing an account of <u>his own</u> mode of operation when he offers an account of the ordinary mode. Philosophic belief, as I have noted, is not ordinary when it pertains to modes of operation. It is advertence to, understanding and judgment of a mode of operation which is not sensible but conscious. Normally, ordinary attention is fixed on the sensible as such or as endowed with meaning. James has overlooked the point that the philosophic account of the ordinary mode cannot be generalized to apply to extraordinary subjects. If he had not overlooked it, he probably would not have been moved to assert that even special men judge the reality of their respective worlds by comparison with the paramount reality of the world of sense.

James' suggestion that the popular mind deals with all of the sub-worlds at one time or another is consistent with his mistaken generalization of ordinary criteria. If it is always the ordinary subject who is present to himself, even though he ventures now and then into extraordinary endeavors, it follows that the reality of extraordinary worlds is dependent upon the approximation of the strength of belief in extraordinary worlds to the strength of ordinary belief. The ontological status of all extraordinary worlds is determined by ordinary criteria, even though ordinary subjects do not engage in ontological reflection. Every subject, whether the popular mind or a special man, is <u>basically ordinary</u> in James' scheme. The stage is set, then, for the emergence of pragmatism as a philosophic doctrine, that is, as an epistemological position to be appealed to for the philosophic purpose of synthesizing or integrating all human endeavors in thought. Ordinary thinking is the paradigm of practical thinking.[61] Insofar as James tends to provide the account of the ordinary mode that an ordinary subject would probably provide if he were so inclined, the pragmatic doctrine that emerges may be suspected immediately of a fundamental inadequacy. The ordinary subject tends to be misled into an emphasis of the sensible, and self-present operations are obscured.[62]

The horizonal structure differs fundamentally from James' scheme. The differences have a common root in James' objectivism. While this conclusion may seem odd in light of James' psychological interests, it remains that his account is entirely in terms of 'worlds'. But worlds constitute only one component of the phenomenon to be investigated. From this objectivism there follows the inadequacy of James' list of sub-worlds. Placing his emphasis upon the objective dimension, James naturally overlooks the subjective dimension, that is, how objects and objectives are dealt with by different types of subjects. Again, all subjects have abstract ideas, whether personally generated or simply borrowed from the existing culural matrix. All subjects have prejudices. Because these two types of object differ from one another, James seems to conclude to two different sub-worlds while implying that there is basically only one type of subject. If James had acknowledged the intrinsic relation of worlds, standpoints, and modes, he might have concluded that abstract ideas and common prejudices do not constitute worlds, and that differences exist not only on the objective side but also on the side of the subject. As James' scheme suffers from objectivism, so quite naturally it suffers from an inattention to the subject. In the objectivist context, this inattention is reinforced by a definition of subjectivity as the interference of arbitrariness with otherwise 'objective' procedures, "mere subjectivity".

James' objectivism is related to the predominance of the ordinary standpoint in his philosophic approach. On the one hand, James affirms that "any relation to our mind at all, in the absence of a stronger relation, suffices to make an object real."[63] Thus far he approximates to the standpoint of the philosopher who has not yet developed the tools to be implemented in a philosophic integration of the variety of human endeavors. The assertion does not reflect an ontological commitment; 'real' is employed heuristically. But James retains the position that the world of sense is the paramount reality. In this respect, James is inadequately philosophic, for he imports into the philosophic horizon criteria proper to the ordinary horizon. There results an account of the range of human endeavors that an ordinary subject might offer if he were so inclined. In contrast, the horizonal structure depends upon a suspension or withholding of judgment upon the philosophic value of criteria employed by any of the other five horizons. The philosophic horizon is a horizon in search of an understanding of criteria-in-operation, while other horizons are implementations of criteria that arise, as it were, in practice. The philosophic horizon is characterized by a suspension of belief in the <u>absolute adequacy</u> of ordinary criteria of reality or any other, while the ordinary horizon, as Schutz has observed, is characterized by a suspension of doubt concerning the absolute adequacy of ordinary criteria of reality.[64] The ordinary criteria about which the ordinary subject as such has no doubt are, first and foremost, the criteria of sensibility, palpability, tangibility -- criteria governing the apprehension of "that which stands opposite".

The horizonal structure is an intelligible, interlocking set of terms and relations that it may be well to have about when it comes to describing internal cultural relations. On the one hand, it brings into relief the horizonal differences which may underlie or simply complicate a variety of contentious and non-contentious human relationships. On the other hand, it is relatively free from the kinds of presuppositions which predetermine the outcomes of investigations of internal cultural relations.

NOTES TO CHAPTER II

[1] See A Dictionary of Sociology, ed. G. Duncan Mitchell (London: Routledge & Kegan Paul, 1968), pp. 182-183.

[2] Ibid., pp. 183-184.

[3] Letter II, 310e.

[4] A fragment from Aristotle's lost dialogue On Kingship affirms this fact while still admitting the possibility of extraordinary influences: "It was not only not necessary for a king to become a philosopher, but actually a hindrance to his work: that, however, it was necessary [for a good king] to listen to the true philosopher and to be agreeable to their advice." The fragment is cited by Hannah Arendt in Between Past and Future, pp. 289-290n.8.

[5] See Marxist Social Thought, ed. Robert Freedman (New York: Harcourt, Brace & World, 1968), pp. 140 ff.

[6] See Theories of Society: Foundations of Modern Sociological Theory, eds. Parsons, Shils, Naegele, Pitts (New York: The Free Press, 1961), p. 538.

[7] Ibid.

[8] See Henri Lefebvre, The Sociology of Marx, trans. Norbert Guterman (New York: Vintage Books, 1969), Chap. 4, especially p. 98.

[9] There is another usage of 'mystical' which is related to the notion of mystification or mysticism in Marxian criticism of ideology. It has a connotation of "privilege-preserving thought" and is not the notion of the mystical employed here. Ownership of the means of production may indeed signal 'mystification' to a Marxist, but it does not imply mysticism or even a less developed form of religiosity. On Marx's notion of ideology, see <u>Marxist Social Thought</u>, pp. 214-215. On his notion of religion, see pp. 227-231.

[10] It was part of the rabbinical tradition that one must have a trade. Consequently, a religious horizon could determine class status in certain milieus.

[11] See Georg Lukacs, <u>History and Class Consciousness</u>, trans. Rodney Livingstone (Cambridge, Mass.: The MIT Press, 1971), pp. 46 ff. on class consciousness.

[12] <u>Marxist Social Thought</u>, pp. 176 ff.

[13] <u>A Dictionary of Sociology</u>, p. 31.

[14] This is not to say, of course, that ordinary subjects seek each other's company, and that artists congregate, simply in virtue of their shared horizons. Groups of ordinary subjects are formed for other reasons as well, such as shared interest in one area of the ordinary world. But in many cases horizonal similarity forms, as it were, a broad context within which group-formation on other bases takes place. Similarly, artistic groups are formed on grounds of style and technique, with horizonal similarity providing the broad context within which styles and techniques are distinguished.

[15] One may also speak of internal horizonal conflicts which may divide the members of a single horizon more or less radically. But, as we shall see in Chapter III, internal horizonal conflicts are normally derivative of conflicts between distinct horizons co-existing in a given cultural matrix.

[16] <u>A Dictionary of Sociology</u>, pp. 138-139.

[17] T. S. Eliot, <u>Christianity and Culture</u> (New York: Harcourt, Brace & World, 1940), pp. 111-112.

[18] <u>Ibid.</u>, p. 117.

[19] <u>Ibid.</u>, p. 119.

[20] <u>Ibid.</u>, p. 95.

[21] <u>Ibid.</u>, pp. 108-110, 95.

[22]Ibid., p. 110.

[23]Ibid., p. 108.

[24]See Karl Mannheim, _Ideology and Utopia_, trans. Louis Wirth and Edward Shils (New York: Harcourt, Brace & World, 1936).

[25]Hans Barth has clearly exposed the self-reversing character of ideology-critique in his _Truth and Ideology_, trans. Frederic Lilge (Berkeley: University of California Press, 1976), pp. 190-194. On p. 192 Barth writes: "To charge consciousness with being ideological requires a prior distinction between "true" and "false" consciousness; and to make this distinction, it is sufficient that a concrete consciousness reckon with the possibility of being affected and restricted by the prevailing social conditions. The mere suspicion of finding oneself in such a situation signals caution in the acceptance of one's own findings. Thus, the insight that one's own knowledge is conditioned is arrived at on the ground that the idea of truth itself is unconditional . . .. It is obvious, however, that if the theory of ideology were applied consistently, no intellectual position could escape the conditioning force of its own interests and would have to allow this dependency to be exposed . . .. We have shown that the reduction of intellectual content to social power is self-defeating." See also Lewis S. Feuer, _Marx and the Intellectuals: A Set of Post-Ideological Essays_ (Garden City: Doubleday, 1969). Feuer notes the "remarkable fact that Marx and Engels provided no theory of the intellectual class," and he exposes the incoherence to which I have alluded in this way: What Marx and Engels did say about intellectuals going over to the proletariat "carries little psychological conviction; it says that quite apart from any personal involvement of emotion, economic interest, or desire for power, the mere understanding of the laws of social development suffices to bring a section of the intellectuals to the proletarian side. As far as intellectuals are concerned, in other words, it affirms that existence does not determine consciousness, but that rather a purely theoretical consciousness determines existence. The revolutionary intellectual evidently then stands with Promethean exceptionalism against the whole materialist conception of history." Again: "A profound dilemma, however, would have confronted Marx and Engels if they had tried to develop a theory of the intellectual class. They would not have been able to do so without abandoning either their materialist conception of history or their idea of the self-emancipation of the working class." See pp. 53-54.

[26]By 'subjective' here is not meant 'arbitrary' as in the phrase "merely subjective". Subjective development is the internal dynamism of a horizon.

[27] As Lonergan notes: "The multiplicity of horizons as [a] philosophic issue arises when we ask: 1. Is some horizon the field, or is there no field? 2. If some horizon is the field, how can it be determined? To deny that there is a field is to deny that philosophy has a positive content; still that denial is itself philosophic though perhaps unconvincingly so. Positivism: Let's do science. Pragmatism: Let's experiment, see what happens. Scepticism: Let's inquire some more. Relativism: Let's face it; there are no definitive answers, just points of view. To affirm that there is a field involves one in the second question which is at once ontological and epistemological. It is ontological in its consequent: beyond such and such a limit there is nothing to be known and so no indocta ignorantia (untutored ignorance). It settles where reality ends and where meaninglessness begins. It is epistemological in its antecedent: to define the field raises the question of the truth of the definition; and the definition is true in virtue of known evidence; what, then, is the evidence? This evidence is of some reality; hence, the second question is ontological also in the antecedent." See his Notes on Existentialism, p. 17.

[28] See Lonergan, A Second Collection, p. 97.

[29] Hegel wrote that "subjectivity sometimes means something wholly idiosyncratic, and at other times something with the highest of claims, since everything which I am to recognize has also the task of becoming mine and attaining validity in me." See his Philosophy of Right, trans. T. M. Knox (London: Oxford University Press, 1967), Additions, p. 232. Lonergan makes a similar distinction of uses in Collection, pp. 237-238.

[30] Lonergan has argued at length that this confrontational notion of an object is rooted in the extroversion of sense perception and that it has nothing whatever to do with the problem of objectivity. See his Insight, pp. 182-184; see also his Understanding and Being: An Introduction and Companion to Insight, eds. Elizabeth A. Morelli and Mark D. Morelli (Toronto, New York: Edwin Mellen Press, 1980), Chap. IV. In full accord with the etymological meaning of 'object' is the intuition principle of Kant's Critique of Pure Reason. As Heidegger has observed, to understand the Critique one must literally hammer into one's mind the principle that knowledge is primarily intuition. See Martin Heidegger, Kant und das Problem der Metaphysik (Frankfurt am Main, 1965), p. 29. See also Giovanni Sala, "The A Priori in Human Knowledge: Kant's Critique of Pure Reason and Lonergan's Insight," The Thomist, Vol. XL, No. 2 (1976), 188-192; and KRV A108-109. For Lonergan's detailed analysis of the 'myth' that knowing is like looking, see his unpublished talk "Consciousness and the Trinity," 1963, The Lonergan Centre, Toronto, pp. 4-5, and Collection, pp. 232-236. On the 'counter-position' that

knowing is something like looking, see his Insight, pp. 253, 320, 321, 406, 412-416, 425, 496, 581-583, 634-635, 646.

[31] Frank Plumpton Ramsey has noted that, in cases where disputes do not seem capable of decisive settlement, "it is a heuristic maxim that the truth lies not in one of the two disputed views but in some third possibility which has not yet been thought of, which we can only discover by rejecting something assumed as obvious by both the disputants." See The Foundations of Mathematics, ed. R. B. Braithwaite (London: Routledge & Kegan Paul, 1931), pp. 115-116. Both subjectivists and objectivists seem to employ the term 'object' in its familiar sense, as "that which stands opposite". My position here is similar to that maintained by R. G. Collingwood in Speculum Mentis, p. 11: "When I call a thing subjective I mean that it is or pertains to a subject or conscious mind. When I call it objective, I mean that it is or pertains to an object of which such a mind is conscious."

[32] Aristotle, Nicomachean Ethics I, V; see also Hannah Arendt, The Human Condition (Garden City: Doubleday, 1959), pp. 13-14.

[33] See Nicholas Lobkowicz, Theory and Practice. History of a Concept from Aristotle to Marx (Notre Dame: University of Notre Dame Press, 1967), pp. 7-8, 26-31; Hannah Arendt, The Human Condition, pp. 13-14; Eric Voegelin, "Reason: The Classic Experience," The Southern Review (July, 1974), 252.

[34] Lobkowicz, Theory and Practice, pp. 3-4.

[35] Ibid., p. 11; Arendt, The Human Condition, p. 13; Richard J. Bernstein, Praxis and Action: Contemporary Philosophies of Human Activity (Philadelphia: University of Pennsylvania Press, 1971), x.

[36] Lobkowicz, Theory and Practice, p. 8.

[37] Arendt, The Human Condition, pp. 15-16.

[38] Aristotle, Politics 1333a30-33, trans. Ernest Barker.

[39] Arendt, The Human Condition, pp. 14-15; Lobkowicz, Theory and Practice, pp. 70-71; Thomas Aquinas, Summa theologiae ii, 2. 179, especially art. 2. See also Arendt, Ibid., p. 17.

[40] See, for example, Julien Benda, The Betrayal of the Intellectuals, trans. Richard Aldington (Boston: Beacon Press, 1955). Benda's criticism of les clercs seems to be entirely in terms of the distinction between contemplation and political involvement.

[41]Lobkowicz, _Theory and Practice_, pp. 29-30.

[42] The oratorical nature of the properly human life suggests that _polis_-life corresponds perhaps to the scholarly horizon at least partly. However, inasmuch as the end of _polis_-life is practical and social, it may be treated as we might treat the political today, that is, as a specialization of the ordinary horizon. See Lonergan, _Insight_, pp. 207-209: "But the practicality of common sense engenders and maintains enormous structures of technology, economics, politics . . .."

[43] See Thomas Luckmann's remarks in _The Structures of the Life-World_, xviii.

[44] A modern scheme, devised by William James, will be considered in the following subsection.

[45]Arendt, _The Human Condition_, p. 17; Eric Voegelin, "Reason: The Classic Experience," 237-264. For more on imperialistic cultural movements, see Chapter III on the notion of totalization.

[46] _Principles of Psychology_ (New York: Henry Holt, 1890), Vol. II, Chap. 21, pp. 291 ff.

[47]_Ibid._, pp. 292-293, 294n.

[48]_Ibid._, pp. 293-294.

[49]_Ibid._, p. 294.

[50] It is in this sense that the model is philosophic, as will be shown in Chapter IV.

[51] _Fichte: Science of Knowledge_ (Wissenschaftslehre), eds. and trans. Peter Heath and John Lachs (New York: Appleton-Century-Croft, 1970), pp. 31-32. See also William James, "The Present Dilemma in Philosophy" in _The Writings of William James_, ed. J. J. McDermott (Chicago, London: University of Chicago Press, 1977), p. 363: "The history of philosophy is to a great extent that of a certain clash of human temperaments. Undignified as such a treatment may seem to some of my colleagues, I shall have to take account of this clash and explain a good many of the divergencies of philosophies by it. Of whatever temperament a professional philosopher is, he tries, when philosophizing, to sink the fact of his temperament. Temperament is no conventionally recognized reason, so he urges impersonal reasons only for his conclusions. Yet his temperament really gives him a stronger bias than any of his more strictly objective premises. It loads the evidence for him one way or the other . . .." See also F. C. S. Schiller, _Must Philosophers Disagree? And Other_

Essays in Popular Philosophy (London: Macmillan, 1934), pp. 10-11: "Actually every philosophy was the offspring, the legitimate offspring, of an idiosyncracy, and the history and psychology of its author had far more to do with its development than der Gang der Sache selbst. Whenever it is possible to reconstruct the psychological history of a philosopher, it plainly attests the truth of this apercu. And the reason why so many philosophies remain mysteries is precisely because we cannot reconstruct the psychology of their authors . . . .. Thus we see that philosophy cannot fulfill its chosen function of unifying experience without including in its synthesis all the idiosyncracies and personalities which the whole affords. Neither can it understand its own history."

[52] That is, while temperament may influence or even determine initially the grounds of synthesis of the variety of horizons, it need not determine the range of horizons which constitutes the philosophic world to be integrated. For example, temperament may dictate that modes of operation be ignored because they are intangible, impalpable, invisible. In this case, the integration of existing horizons will take the form of an integration of worlds alone, in a limited sense, that is, of worlds conceived apart from their self-present dimensions. Despite temperamental disposition, and despite the related theory of consciousness, the range of data to be accounted for remains the same. What I am suggesting here, with regard to the philosopher's role, is that since temperamental disposition and its philosophic consequences become accessible to the philosophizing subject in the conscious performance of his investigations, the philosopher may transcend temperamental limitations through self-critical attention to the data to be investigated and integrated. While the character of our activities depends upon the quality of our dispositions, it is also true, as Aristotle has remarked, that the quality of our dispositions depends upon the quality of our activities. See his Nicomachean Ethics II. i. 8. See also Nicholas Rescher, "Philosophical Disagreement," The Review of Metaphysics, Vol. XXXII, No. 2 (Dec. 1978), 227: "It is, however, important to recognize that such evaluative predispositions need by no means always prevail in our reasoning. One may be forced in a certain direction of credence in spite of and notwithstanding one's inclinations in another . . . .. The presumptions at issue are like most legal presumptions in being defeasible--liable to be upset or reversed by sufficiently weighty counterindications. A probative orientation exerts a certain cognitive pressure, but its force is not infinite and irresistible but can be dampened and even ultimately deflected and redirected. Accordingly, such orientations are not necessarily something fixed and immutable."

[53] Alfred Schutz has taken over James' conception of the paramount reality, extending it to explicitly include not only

66

physical objects apprehended by external perception but also cultural objects apprehended as already endowed with meaning. See The Structures of the Life-World, p. 6. Schutz's notion of everyday reality is virtually identical with the notion of the ordinary world, except that the horizon of experience is contracted to include only sensible and cultural objects. Note also that this broader notion of the ordinary world is related to the problem of the relation of scholarship to the ordinary horizon; for the scholar deals continuously with meaning-endowed objects. See Lonergan, Method in Theology, pp. 233–234.

[54]James, Principles of Psychology, Vol. II, p. 301.

[55]See Lonergan, Insight, pp. 74–76 on the canon of operations in empirical science.

[56]See Richard E. Palmer, Hermeneutics (Evanston: Northwestern University Press, 1969), Chap. 4; four styles of contemporary sociology have been distinguished by Gibson Winter in Elements for a Social Ethic (New York, 1966).

[57] See Lonergan, Insight, Chaps. II–V, especially pp. 198 and 294 where the doubt is expressed.

[58]See Schutz and Luckmann, The Structures of the Life-World, p. 22.

[59] James' emphasis of ordinary criteria is apparently supported by several facts. The success of natural science and its apparent reliance upon ordinary criteria of reality (conceived perhaps too narrowly as sensible consequences) have given weight to the assumption of the ultimacy of ordinary criteria, as has the natural scientific preference for natural over cultural objects. But, as Eddington's well-known reflections on his two tables suggest, sensible consequences are sometimes far removed from immediate apprehension of sensible objects. Ordinary and scientific modes of operation differ; an actual failure to provide an adequate account of this difference and to communicate the account adequately seems to lie at the root of the persistent conflict between the scientific and the ordinary apprehensions of the universe of being that has existed at least since the Renaissance. If this conflict seems to have abated, this is not because a solution has been discovered and generally accepted. Its latency seems rather to be the result of what Einstein called positively liberating technological effects of science on human affairs. The perpetual relevance of practicality has also given weight to James' assumption that ordinary criteria of reality are relevant to the task of evaluating the reality of sub-worlds proper to extraordinary horizons. A distinction may be drawn between perpetual short-term relevance

and perpetual long-term relevance. Natural scientists claim for their activities and conclusions a perpetual long-term relevance which the ordinary subject, in virtue of his horizonal limitations, does not easily apprehend. Certainly, the ordinary subject acknowledges the long-term relevance of science as a mode of operation inasmuch as he believes what scientists say; but the acknowledgement is not immanently generated, that is, it is not a function of his own mode and standpoint. Historians also claim perpetual long-term relevance for their activities which the ordinary subject as such does not explicitly acknowledge. See Sir Arthur Eddington, The Nature of the Physical World (Cambridge: Cambridge University Press, 1928), xi-xix; also his New Pathways in Science (Cambridge: Cambridge University Press, 1947), p. 1. See Lonergan, Insight, p. 294 on the Renaissance conflict of science and common sense. On the background of this conflict in the Galilean distinction between primary and secondary qualities, see E. A. Burtt, The Metaphysical Foundations of Modern Science (Garden City: Doubleday, 1954), Chap. III, Section C. For Einstein's reflections, see Philosophy for a Time of Crisis, ed. Adrienne Koch (New York: E. P. Dutton, 1960), pp. 97-100. The notion of relevance is treated at length and in detail, in a Husserlian context, by Alfred Schutz in Reflections on the Problem of Relevance, ed. Richard M. Zaner (New Haven, London: Yale University Press, 1970). See also Lonergan, "Aquinas Today: Tradition and Innovation," 166: "The variations of the boundary of one's knowledge and interests, in extent, intensity, and selectivity help fill out what we mean by relevance. The relevant in an absolute sense is what is known, what is of interest, what may be selected for attention and consideration."

[60]James, Principles of Psychology, Vol. II, p. 301.

[61]On the dominance of the pragmatic motive in James' conception of the mind's selectivity, see Schutz, Reflections on the Problem of Relevance, pp. 5-6.

[62] Whether this is in fact the manner in which pragmatism emerged as a philosophic doctrine would have to be determined by historical studies of some complexity. Again, whether pragmatism is actually characterized by the inadequacy that would seem to follow from the emergence would have to be determined by similar studies. My purpose has been to illustrate the limits applicable to a philosophic use of James' notion of belief, given its foundation in his account of the ordinary mode of operation. The interested reader may consult Arthur Lovejoy, who has distinguished thirteen versions of pragmatism. See Pragmatic Philosophy, ed. Amelie Rorty (Garden City: Anchor Books, 1966), pp. 339-341. See also, John E. Smith, The Spirit of American Philosophy (Oxford: Oxford University Press, 1963), pp.

187-214. Smith concludes that thinkers in the American milieu hold (i) that thinking is primarily an activity in response to a concrete situation aimed at solving problems, and (ii) that ideas and theories must "make a difference" in the conduct of the living thinker and in his situation. But American philosophy as a whole cannot be affirmed to be reliant upon merely practical or purely practical self-presence on the basis of this description alone. The issue must be decided by cases, and in each case it will be decided by (i) the narrowness or breadth of the notions of "concrete situation" and 'problem', and (ii) the narrowness or breadth of the relevance-structure determining what ideas possibly do or do not "make a difference".

[63]James, Principles of Psychology, Vol. II, p. 299.

[64] Schutz and Luckmann, The Structures of the Life-World, p. 36. See also E. Husserl, Ideas, p. 86: "The right attitude to take in the pre-philosophical and, in a good sense, dogmatic sphere of inquiry, to which all the empirical sciences (but not these alone) belong, is in full consciousness to discard all scepticism together with all "natural philosophy" and "theory of knowledge," and find the data of knowledge there where they actually face you, whatever difficulties epistemological reflection may subsequently raise concerning the possibility of such data being there."

III

HORIZONAL CONSTELLATIONS

The purpose of the present chapter is to introduce into the horizonal structure an anticipation
of the types of dynamic relationships into which
co-existing horizons may enter. Chapter I was in
part a response to Markarian's suggestion that a
methodological approach to the study of culture be
three-dimensional. In the present chapter I shall
attempt to move beyond a consideration of basic components of the horizonal structure by surveying typical relations of horizons to one another and typical
configurations of sets of co-existing horizons. In
this way, the model may be expanded to take into
account the material dynamism of the object it is
employed to investigate.

It should be recalled that my concern is to
provide a model which may be helpful to students
of culture and especially to disorientated philosophers seeking a responsible course of action. It
is the task of the student of culture to determine
the factual relations into which horizons happen
to have entered in a given historical period. It
is the task of the synthesizing philosopher, guided
by a concern to integrate human endeavors in thought,
to determine fundamentally the relations of co-existing horizons to one another. It is the task of the
disorientated philosopher to obtain a grasp of the
factual configuration of the milieu in which he finds
himself and in which he is to operate responsibly.
The present task is the preparatory investigation
which is to provide further details of the heuristic
structure which may be employed to achieve these
determinate understandings.

1. CONSTELLATIONS

A constellation of horizons is a group, set, or cluster of distinct horizons of subjects who are at least present to one another and who may be understood and known as horizons by one another. Constellations of horizons may be simple or complex, potential or actual, incomplete, microcosmically complete or complete.

1.1. SIMPLE OR COMPLEX

By a simple constellation is meant a set of two distinct horizons of mutually present subjects. Most frequently, a simple constellation is constituted by the ordinary horizon and one extraordinary horizon. When a scientist and a man of common sense find themselves seated together on a train, there is a simple constellation. Again, when a psychoanalyst sits down to dinner with his ordinary spouse, a simple constellation is formed. But simple constellations may also be constituted by two distinct extraordinary horizons. Thus there is a simple constellation when, the man of common sense having departed, the scientist is joined by a scholar, an artist, a philosopher, or a religious subject.

A complex constellation is a set of three or more distinct horizons of mutually present sujects. Thus we have a complex constellation of horizons when the scientist and the scholar are joined by a philosopher, a man of common sense, an artist, or a religious subject. Similarly, a complex constellation exists if they are joined by all four. Again, a constellation becomes complex when the psychoanalyst and the ordinary spouse are joined by a scholar. The significance of the distinction between simple and complex constellations will become apparent when I turn to a consideration of typical relationships of co-existing horizons.

1.2. POTENTIAL OR ACTUAL

A potential constellation is a simple or complex constellation in which the mutual presence of the member horizons has not yet been made problematic by the emergence in at least one of the members of a recognition of horizonal dissonance. By a recognition of horizonal dissonance is meant a determinate and articulate or indeterminate or indirectly expressed apprehension of differences between standpoints, modes of operation, and worlds. If a man of common sense and a scientist pass their time playing cards, the simple constellation is merely potential. Their mutual presence could be made problematic by a recognition of horizonal dissonance, but this recognition has not emerged. However, if their conversation turns to a topic which bears extraordinary treatment, an actual constellation is in the making. A set of two commonsense subjects is not a potential constellation. While topics may arise which bear extraordinary treatment, de facto no extraordinary subject is present. On the other hand, a set constituted by one ordinary subject and one scientific subject is a potential constellation. A scientific subject is present to deal scientifically with those emergent topics which bear scientific treatment. Again, a set constituted by two extraordinary subjects, one scientific and the other religious, is a potential constellation. As the conversation turns from everyday issues to the question of miracles, for example, different extraordinary modes of operation are called forth and a recognition of horizonal dissonance may emerge. Every constellation is potential inasmuch as one of the member subjects may diverge from ordinary operations in virtue of previous extraordinary development, but in fact does not. A potential constellation becomes virtually actual as one or more of its member subjects diverge from the ordinary mode of operation in virtue of the introduction of a topic which bears extraordinary treatment. A constellation is fully actual if the mutual presence of the members has become problematic in virtue of the emergence in at least one of the members of a recognition of horizonal dissonance.

1.3. COMPLETENESS

A constellation may be incomplete, microcosmically complete, or complete. The completeness or incompleteness of a constellation is determined by adverting to the number and kinds of horizons constitutive of a given cultural matrix. For example, it is commonly assumed that the practical and the religious horizons were the only horizons constitutive of very early cultures.[1] A microcosmically complete constellation, then, would be the simple constellation composed of one ordinary and one religious subject,

73

and no incomplete constellation would be possible.
In our culture, on the other hand, there are at least
six distinct horizons (five basic combinations and
the ordinary horizon). The microcosmically complete
constellation may be a set constituted by at least
one ordinary, one artistic, one scientific, one philosophic, one scholarly, and one religious subject.
Any simple constellation is incomplete; some complex
constellations may be microcosmically complete. A
complete constellation is any given cultural matrix
considered as the set of mutually present sets of
subjects of distinct standpoints, modes of operation,
and worlds. This notion of completeness gives rise
to a question regarding the nature of mutual presence.

1.3.1. MUTUAL PRESENCE AND COMPLETENESS

Mutual face-to-face presence is not a necessary
condition for a potential constellation. Mutual presence must be conceived more broadly if the notion
of a cultural matrix is to remain meaningful. Horizons
are present to one another inasmuch as their various
objectifications lie within the experiential range
of the variety of subjects constitutive of a cultural
matrix. Subjects express themselves, they objectify
their horizons in written as well as spoken language,
in lasting productions, in perduring organizations
and institutions. As a cultural matrix is constituted
by the existing variety of horizons, so also is it
permeated by the self-expression of the existing
variety. The meaning expressed is carried by objectifications and it has a relatively permanent presence
even in the absence of the originating subjects.[2]
The meaning lies within the experiential range of
subjects inasmuch as they live among the carriers
and are informed and directed by them. Even in the
relative solitude of an absence of face-to-face encounters, a recognition of horizonal dissonance may
emerge. If an ordinary subject confronts a carrier
of scientific meaning, a potential simple constellation exists; if a scientific subject confronts a
carrier of religious meaning, we have a potential
simple constellation. If an artist, an ordinary subject, and a scientist confront in relative solitude
one another's self-expressions, there exists a potential complex constellation. Finally, if commonsense,
scientific, artistic, scholarly, philosophic, and
religious subjects are confronting each others' objectifications recurrently and frequently, there exists

a perduring potential constellation which is complete, a cultural matrix similar to our own. In cases where mutual presence is not the face-to-face presence of subjects to one another, the transition from potentiality to actuality is effected by means of the attempts of subjects to go beyond mere experience of objectifications to understand them. These attempts lead to a recognition of horizonal dissonance inasmuch as they are actuations of horizon-specific modes of operation with regard to differently horizon-specific expressions of meaning.[3]

1.4. RELEVANT DATA

The student of culture concerned to understand the existing cultural matrix and its factual internal relations, and the philosopher concerned to orientate himself in the present culture, must take as their common object of inquiry a complex, actual, and complete constellation. The constellation must be complex; for our culture is constituted by more than two horizons. It must be actual; for a merely potential constellation is not revelatory of horizonal relations. Internal cultural relations come to light as sets of ordinarily-operative subjects are transformed by the emergence of extraordinary operations in one or more of the members. Finally, the constellation must be complete; for only a study of the relations of the full range of existing horizons in their native states will answer the question posed by the student of culture and supply the philosopher with an adequate appreciation of the actual <u>context</u> of his endeavors. The student of contemporary culture and the disorientated philosopher cannot be content to examine critically only their face-to-face encounters or to observe carefully only a microcosmically complete constellation. They must attend to their entire cultural milieu as a self-expressing set of sets of mutually present horizons and discover in it the dynamic configuration of their age.

The present aim, on the other hand, is to expand the horizonal structure introduced in Chapter I by constructing a typology of dynamic relations of horizons to one another. Accordingly, every actual constellation -- whether it is simple, complex but incomplete, microcosmically complete, or the complete constellation -- is data relevant to the task at hand.

1.4.1. THE RANGE OF INTERSUBJECTIVE COMBINATIONS

The mathematically possible basic combinations of horizons in single subjects have already been surveyed. As basic combinations pertain to single subjects, so intersubjective combinations pertain to constellations of horizons. Types of subjects combine with one another in a variety of ways. The basic range of possible intersubjective combinations of horizons may be represented heuristically by constructing a matrix [see Fig. 1]. By using the matrix as a guide, the student of culture and the disorientated philosopher may pursue an understanding of the dynamic configuration of their culture. But the matrix may also be employed in the present context to guide the construction of a typology of relationships of co-existing horizons to one another.

The matrix is representative of only the basic range of possible intersubjective combinations, for its elements are the five basic combinations and the ordinary horizon. It represents twenty-one bodies of intersubjective expression. Fifteen of these are relevant to the exposition of actual relations between extraordinary subjects, and five are relevant to the exposition of actual relations between ordinary and extraordinary subjects. Of the twenty-one, six are especially relevant to an exposition of relations between subjects sharing the same horizon.

Additional matrices can be constructed to represent further ranges of bodies of intersubjective expression. The further ranges can be determined by exploiting the full range of possible combinations of horizons in single subjects [see Chapter I, Section 9.3.]. For example, triple combinations can be combined with double combinations, single combinations with fourfold combinations, and so on; and these relations could be explored. However, it would have to be kept in mind by the investigator that not all additional matrices will be relevant to every study of historical periods. The entire range of matrices is relevant to the study of horizonal relations in the present and, assuming the maintenance of the present level of complexity of human endeavor, it will be relevant to studies of future configurations as well. The elements of the horizonal structure have been determined by adverting to the number and kinds of horizons existing at the present time. Moreover, the range of possibilities represented by the

FIGURE 1

THE BASIC RANGE OF INTERSUBJECTIVE COMBINATIONS

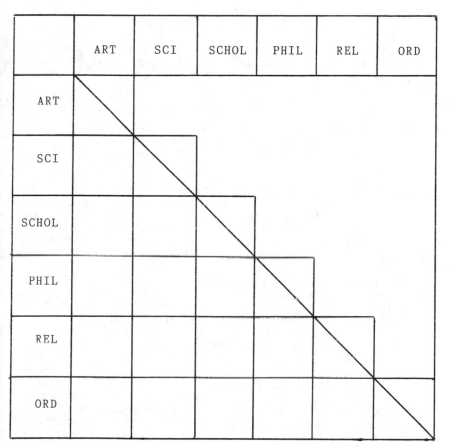

21 Basic Intersubjective Combinations: 15 extraordinary
bodies of expression; 6 self-referential bodies of expression; 5 combined bodies of ordinary and extraordinary expression.

basic matrix and all additional matrices is not to be taken as an exhaustive representation of combinations possible in the future. As the six basic horizons have emerged in time, so further horizons could emerge. The basic matrix represents schematically the existing complete constellation. It is of sufficient complexity for an exposition of types of horizonal relations, an investigation of actual horizonal relations, and for the contextualization of present-day philosophic activity.

2. TYPICAL RELATIONSHIPS

Horizonal relations are functions of efforts made by subjects with different horizons to accommodate the perplexity generated by recognitions of horizonal dissonance.

Horizonal dissonance, and the horizonal multiplicity in which it is based, are perplexing. Every horizon is a more or less integrated unity of a standpoint, mode of operation, and world; and this unity, if not known, is at least self-present. As potential constellations become actual, the self-present unity of horizons is threatened. There are many horizons, and each one is a unity. If the emergent perplexity were given explicit expression, it might take the form of a question of this type: How can the existence of a multiplicity of horizons be reconciled with the self-present unity of my own horizon?

Internal horizonal perplexity is related to the twofold orientation of horizons. On the one hand, the subject of a particular horizon is determinately directed by horizon-specific ideals; he is a man of common sense, an artist, a scientist, a scholar, a philosopher, or a religious man. On the other hand, every subject is indeterminately directed by the ideals of human subjectivity in general; while each of us has a horizon, each of us is also a human being. Now, a determinate mode of operation from a determinate standpoint with regard to a determinate range of objects and objectives may or may not be a partial realization of the ideals of human subjectivity in general. Normally, the development of a horizon is attended by an identification, more or less complete and more or less deliberate, of the ideals proper to the emergent horizon with the ideals of human subjectivity in general. The identification may be

78

expressed linguistically or merely performatively. The developing scientist, for example, tends naturally to identify his emergent standpoint, mode, and world with the adequate standpoint, the adequately objective mode, and the universe of being. This identification commonly takes place despite the problem posed for every extraordinary subject by his own recurrent return to the ordinary horizon.[4] It seems to have its root in the apparently self-validating unity of the developing horizon. As potential constellations become actual, the natural identification is temporarily dissolved; other apparently self-validating unities are recognized to exist. The adequacy of the identification is called into question: Are my world, mode, and standpoint coincident with the universe of being, the adequately objective mode of operation, and the basic ideals of human subjectivity in general?

The subject of a horizon exists in a tension between determinate horizon-specific ideals and the indeterminate and over-reaching ideals of human subjectivity in general. The ideals of human subjectivity in general point beyond any determinate world, surface mode, or standpoint. Their over-reaching nature is revealed inasmuch as one adverts to the process of over-reaching by recurrent questioning which is constitutive of horizonal development and as well to the variable range of perduring horizons. In a sense, every horizon is an open-ended unity, and every complete constellation may become still more complex. If this were not the case, horizons would not develop, and a variety of horizons would not perdure.

The existence of the twofold orientation of horizons is naturally revealed by the more explicit expressions of horizonal perplexity. I have already mentioned the problem of the identity of worlds. It is a problem because a distinction is drawn between the worlds of distinct horizons and the universe of being towards which human subjectivity consciously and intentionally tends. The worlds of distinct horizons are determinate ranges of objects and objectives; but the universe of being may or may not include these determinate ranges, and horizonal development reflects the very basic assumption that it goes beyond any determinate range. Again, internal horizonal perplexity may be explicitly formulated as the problem of the identity of modes. This is a problem because a distinction is drawn between the surface modes of distinct horizons and a deep mode of operation

79

which is taken to be proportionate to the universe
of being. The modes of operation of distinct horizons
are determinate patterned sequences of conscious
and intentional operation; but the deep mode may
or may not inform surface modes, or it may inform
them only partially or inadequately. The structured
anticipation which is any surface mode may or may
not coincide with the heuristic anticipation of the
universe of being in one of its aspects. Again, internal horizonal perplexity may be explicitly formulated
as the problem of the identity of standpoints. This
is a problem because a distinction is drawn between
horizon-specific standpoints and the ideals constitutive of human subjectivity in general. The horizon-
specific ideals are determinate guiding orientations;
but the ideals of human subjectivity are over-reaching.

The notions of a universe of being, a deep mode
of operation, and ideals of human subjectivity in
general, taken together, constitute the heuristic
notion of the basic horizon of human existence.[5]
If an account of this horizon were acquired, and
if the account were also generally known, a culture
would be in possession of the ultimate frame of reference for the fully adequate intellectual integration
of the variety of human endeavors. However, inasmuch
as an ultimate frame of reference does not orientate
human endeavors relative to one another at the present
time, at least explicitly, subjects have no ultimate
court of appeal to which they may turn to alleviate
the perplexity generated by recognitions of horizonal
dissonance and multiplicity. Consequently, attempts
to accommodate internal horizonal perplexity take
a variety of forms, rather than a single form, and
they give rise to a limited variety of types of intersubjective relationships.

2.1. IDEALS OF CULTURAL UNITY

The range of relationships into which co-existing
horizons enter in actual constellations is limited.
As constellations are actualized, member subjects
acquire a new or renewed awareness of the distinction
between horizon-specific ideals and the ideals of
human subjectivity in general. As horizonal integrity
is called into question, so also is the presumed
coincidence of horizon-specific ideals and the ideals
of human subjectivity in general. Once horizonal
perplexity has emerged and the normal identification

of horizon-specific ideals with the ideals of human subjectivity in general has been dissolved, efforts to accommodate perplexity are governed by one or the other of two possible ideals of cultural unity.

By a cultural ideal or ideal of cultural unity is meant a more or less articulate conception of the unity of the variety of co-existing human endeavors. There seem to be two fundamental cultural ideals, corresponding approximately to two different notions of unity. Georg Simmel, in his study of conflict, has distinguished between two notions of unity, and one of these notions is useful in the present context.

We designate as "unity" the consensus and concord of interacting individuals, as against their discords, separations, and disharmonies. But we also call "unity" the total group-synthesis of persons, energies, and forms, that is, the ultimate wholeness of that group, a wholeness which covers both strictly-speaking unitary relations and dualistic relations.[6]

The first notion of unity is concrete. The second is an abstract notion of unity, the unity which is a cultural matrix regardless of the degree of concrete unity attained by its members; it corresponds to my notion of the complete constellation. A further, concrete notion of unity may be distinguished, the reductive unity of a cultural matrix which is neither a unity born of consensus and harmony nor the abstract unity of the matrix regardless of the concrete unity attained by its members. Corresponding to the first notion of unity is <u>the ideal of differentiated unity</u> or the ideal of a harmonious blending of elements which retain their individual autonomy and integrity. Corresponding to the third notion of unity is <u>the reductionist ideal of cultural unity</u> or the ideal of a concrete unity which emerges as a result of the annihilation or relegation to inferior positions of all but one of the elements.

Internal horizonal perplexity is accommodated by appealing to these ideals and by entering into relationships under their governance. Pursuit of the reductionist ideal involves either a reversion to the original identification of horizon-specific ideals with the ideals of human subjectivity in general or a transformation of the original identification

81

through the introduction of a new determinate member. That is, the pursuit of the reductionist ideal results either in claims of hegemony for one's own horizon in a given constellation or in the attribution of authoritative status to some other horizon in the same constellation. Guided by the reductionist ideal, the perplexed subject mitigates his perplexity by arrogating to his own horizon the ruling or authoritative position in the constellation of which he is a member, or he supports the arrogation of some other co-existing horizon. On the other hand, pursuit of the ideal of differentiated unity involves a concerted effort to preserve the autonomy of each of the co-existing horizons by resistance against the natural tendency to identify the ideals of human subjectivity in general with the determinate ideals of one horizon in a given constellation. Guided by the collaborative ideal, the perplexed subject mitigates his perplexity by granting equal status to every horizon in the given constellation. However, neither pursuit of the reductionist ideal nor pursuit of the collaborative ideal fully eliminates the tension which is brought to consciousness by the dissolution of natural identification.

Conduct guided by either of the cultural ideals is, so to speak, blind. Conduct guided by the reductionist ideal is blind to the possible existence of fundamental ideals of human subjectivity in general, and this blindspot leads to a renewal of identification or its transformation. Conduct guided by the ideal of differentiated unity is blind inasmuch as the ideals of human subjectivity in general, to which appeal is made implicitly or explicitly, are indeterminate and over-reaching; the fundamental ideals are not perspicuously grasped. However, the former blindness is accompanied by a denial of the existence of that which is not seen, while the latter is qualified by an affirmation of the existence of something (X) which lies beyond any determinate horizon.

Ideals of cultural unity may guide efforts to accommodate internal perplexity even though they remain for the most part implicit and unexpressed. Normally, in fact, cultural ideals are appealed to only implicitly. On the one hand, there is an inherent difficulty in the attempt to express clearly and precisely the ideal of differentiated unity because its formulation requires an appeal to the over-reaching ideals of subjectivity in general. On the other hand, explicit expression is attained more easily by subjects guided by the reductionist ideal because its formulation is bounded by a reference to the determinate ideals of some existing horizon. However, the reductionist ideal may also remain implicit, despite its greater accessibility; for the explicit formulation of horizon-specific ideals requires an unusual shift of attention from the world of one's own horizon to the standpoint, mode, and world of one's own or some other horizon. The implicitness of the ideals does not prevent their effective governance of intersubjective relations. Just as the artist is able to function successfully without a precise conception of the ideal of adequacy governing his artistic activity, so the intersubjective activity constitutive of an actual constellation may be governed by ideals of cultural unity even though none of the members has succeeded in expressing these guiding ideals precisely.

The two guiding ideals constitute the poles of the tension out of which six basic types of intersubjective activity, relating co-existing horizons to one another, emerge. These are the activities of annihilating totalization, relegating totalization, self-abandoning capitulation, subservient capitulation, collaboration, and resistance. In the following subsection I shall define these six terms; secondly, I shall consider simple and complex constellations governed (i) solely by the ideal of differentiated unity, (ii) solely by the reductionist ideal of cultural unity, and (iii) by a mixture of the two ideals; finally, I shall touch briefly on internal horizonal relations. In the course of these discussions I shall offer a few illustrations which may aid the reader in his attempt to understand how the model can be applied by the student of culture and the disorientated philosopher. But the illustrations are intended to be taken at their face-value. They are not investigative conclusions but only devices to facilitate the apprehension of the types of constellations that may emerge. Investigative conclusions are to be sought by the student of culture and the disorientated philosopher seeking a responsible course of action. A preparatory maneuver is undertaken with the positions of the enemy in mind, but it is not itself the engagement of the enemy's main force. The reader may find additional illustrations in the accompanying notes.

83

2.2. RELATIONSHIPS

Horizons are related to one another in actual constellations by subjective activity. By subjective activity is not meant biased, one-sided or partial activity but activity of a conscious and intentional subject who may be "merely subjective" or "adequately objective" in his operations. There are six significant types of subjective activity by which horizons may be related to one another in actual constellations. In the present subsection I shall define generally the terms employed to designate these types. In the following subsection I shall consider the intersubjective combinations of horizons operating in these six ways and provide elucidating illustrations.

2.2.1. TOTALIZATION

By totalization is meant activity aimed at the reduction of a multiplicity of horizons to a monolithic or uniform unity and also the enforcement of that uniform unity by authoritarian means if and when it is attained. There are two types of totalization, <u>annihilating totalization</u> [Tot(A)] and <u>relegating totalization</u> [Tot(R)].' By annihilating totalization is meant activity aimed at the complete destruction, elimination, reduction to non-existence, or abolishment of all horizons except one's own in a given constellation. By relegating totalization is meant activity aimed at the banishment or consignment to an obscure, inferior or 'lower' position in a constellation of all but one's own horizon.[8]

2.2.2. CAPITULATION

By capitulation is meant the activity of acquiescing, yielding, submitting, deferring, or giving up all resistance to the totalizing activity of a co-existing horizon. There are two types of capitulation, <u>self-abandoning capitulation</u> [Cap(A)] and <u>subservient capitulation</u> [Cap(S)].

By self-abandoning capitulation is meant the activity of a horizon that is totally self-forsaking, self-deserting, or yielding in the face of a co-existing totalizing horizon. Self-abandoning capitulation and annihilating totalization are complementary activities. Self-abandoning capitulation is a gradual or rapid relinquishment of horizonal integrity. By subservient capitulation, on the other hand, is meant the activity of a horizon that is servile, subordinating itself to a co-existing totalizing horizon. Subservient capitulation and relegating totalization are complementary activities. Subservient capitulation is a gradual or rapid relinquishment of horizonal autonomy.

2.2.3. COLLABORATION AND RESISTANCE

By collaboration is meant working with others in joint intellectual efforts, in joint practical efforts, or in joint intellectual and practical efforts. There is one type of collaboration [Col]. By resistance [Res] is meant the activity of working against, fighting off, actively opposing or contesting the totalizing and capitulating efforts of co-existing horizons. It is collaboration transformed by the presence of an external threat to the autonomy or integrity of one's own horizon and co-existing horizons in a given constellation.

2.3. TYPES OF ACTUAL CONSTELLATIONS

I shall turn now to a consideration of simple, complex, and complete constellations governed (i) solely by the collaborative ideal, (ii) solely by the reductionist ideal, and (iii) by a mixture of the two ideals. There are three significant types of actual constellations: collaborative, reductionist, and heterogeneous.

2.3.1. COLLABORATIVE CONSTELLATIONS

There is one type of relation characteristic of constellations governed solely by the ideal of differentiated unity: collaboration [Col]. Pursuit of the ideal of differentiated unity involves a concerted effort to preserve the autonomy and integrity of one's own horizon and co-existing horizons by resisting the natural tendency to identify the ideals of a specific horizon with the ideals of human subjectivity in general. If the dissolution of the identification, which follows from the actualization of a constellation, is successfully enforced by every co-existing horizon in a given constellation, the

85

mitigation of horizonal perplexity takes the form of collaborative activity and the constellation as a whole may be named collaborative.

A simple constellation governed solely by the ideal of differentiated unity may take one form. A complex constellation with three member horizons may take one form. The complete constellation, with six member horizons, may take one form [See Chart 1]. In collaborative constellations a member horizon is related to all co-existing horizons by its collaborative activity. While collaborative constellations are constituted solely by collaborators, there is still room for significant differences arising from differences in conceptions of the canons and aims pertinent to collaborative activity in particular instances. The member horizons do not necessarily possess the mutual understanding and self-understanding which would eliminate all intersubjective tensions related to horizonal differences. The level of intersubjective tension in a collaborative constellation may vary considerably because presence differs from knowledge and self-presence differs from self-knowledge. Moreover, besides the intersubjective horizonal tension rooted in differences in the conception of canons and aims in particular instances, there may also be a variable level of intersubjective tension rooted in the fact that even shared canons and aims are pursued and realized in a variety of sequences at a variety of rates.

Collaborative constellations are not easily identified and illustrations are not easily provided. If the investigator is totalizing his own horizon, he will seek evidence of collaboration under the governance of the reductionist ideal. Accordingly, evidence of collaboration will be apprehended initially as evidence of the totalizing subject's failure to realize his cultural ideal. Subsequently, collaborative activity may be apprehended as a misguided effort to realize an unrealizable ideal. The totalizing investigator is likely to be selectively inattentive to data that is not directly relevant to the realization of his preferred ideal. Similarly, if the investigator is capitulating to the totalization of a co-existing horizon, he is likely to apprehend collaborative activity as reasonable cooperation with an aggressor or invader. Genuine collaboration may be misapprehended under the guidance of reductionist anticipations, or, if accurately apprehended,

86

CHART 1

CONSTELLATIONS GOVERNED BY THE IDEAL

OF DIFFERENTIATED UNITY

Simple Constellations

1) Col & Col

Complex Constellations (3 Members)

1) Col & Col & Col

The Complete Constellation

1) Col & Col & Col & Col & Col & Col

———————

it may be seen again as an effort to realize an un-realizable ideal. These possible interferences with cultural investigations may complicate attempts to understand the terms and relations constitutive of the model as well. As adequate investigative activity requires a disinterested and detached stance, so an adequate grasp of the model presently under con-struction requires a detached and disinterested view of the two ideals and their implications for horizonal relations.[9] If this stance has been effectively ap-propriated, illustrations may be effectively clarifica-tory. With this in mind, one may consider the recent emergence of interdisciplinary studies and inter-disciplinary efforts to plan curricula. However, it should be noted that the dominant curricular divi-sions reflect horizonal differences only imperfectly. As classes are distinguished by adverting to economic criteria, so disciplinary divisions are normally made on the basis of differences between subject-matters, objects, and objectives, and little attention is paid to differences between modes of operation and standpoints. Existing curricular divisions are normally the explicit determinants of interdiscipli-nary relations;[10] curriculum planners do not employ explicitly the criteria of horizonal differences.

More specific illustrations of expression gov-erned by a collaborative ideal may be offered. Newman, for example, affirmed the independence of distinct human pursuits in a way that reflects the resolution of internal perplexity by an appeal to the collabora-tive ideal.

> Things which can bear to be cut off from everything else and yet persist in living must have life in themselves; pursuits, which issue in nothing, and still maintain their ground for ages, which are regarded as admirable, though they have not as yet proved themselves to be useful, must have their sufficient end in themselves, whatever it turn out to be.[11]

Again, Jacques Barzun has described the delicate balance between ordinary and extraordinary which he believes must be maintained if a constellation is not to become dangerously contentious.

> Thus the greatest danger to a democratic state is probably the contamination of its politics by Intellect. At the same time, the sound instinct

which keeps apart the work of Intellect and the
work of government can turn into an anti-intellectualism that is equally dangerous to both.[12]

Thoughtful reflection on collaborative combinations
[See Chart 1] may aid the reader further in his personal search for clarifying illustrations. Some possibilities are especially evocative in virtue of
their notable difference from the types of constellations normally encountered. For example, a collaborative (natural) scientific horizon may be combined
with a collaborative religious horizon, or a set
of collaborative extraordinary horizons may be combined with a collaborative ordinary horizon.

2.3.2. REDUCTIONIST CONSTELLATIONS

There are four types of relations characteristic
of constellations governed solely by the reductionist
ideal: annihilating totalization [Tot(A)], relegating
totalization [Tot(R)], self-abandoning capitulation
[Cap(A)], and subservient capitulation [Cap(S)].[13]
The reinforcement of an original identification of
one's horizon-specific ideals with the ideals of
subjectivity in general results in claims of hegemony
in the constellation. From this position there follow
totalizing movements. The shift, subsequent to the
emergence of perplexity, to a new identification
of the horizon-specific ideals of a co-existing horizon with the ideals of human subjectivity in general
results in claims of hegemony for a co-existing horizon other than one's own. From this position there
follow capitulating movements.

A simple constellation governed solely by the
reductionist ideal may take seven forms. A complex
constellation with three member horizons may take
sixteen forms. The complete constellation, with six
member horizons, may take fifty-two forms [See Chart
2]. There can be no capitulating activity in a reductionist constellation without the presence of at
least one totalizing horizon, but totalization may
occur without capitulation. Moreover, in a complex
constellation, if more than one horizon is totalizing,
co-existing capitulators choose from among the totalizing horizons that horizon to which they will grant
hegemony in self-abandoning or merely subservient
fashion.

CHART 2

CONSTELLATIONS GOVERNED BY THE IDEAL

OF REDUCTIONIST UNITY

Simple Constellations

1) Tot(A) & Tot(A)
2) Tot(A) & Tot(R)
3) Tot(R) & Tot(R)
4) Tot(A) & Cap(S)
5) Tot(A) & Cap(A)
6) Tot(R) & Cap(S)
7) Tot(R) & Cap(A)

Complex Constellations (3 Members)

1) Tot(A) & Tot(A) & Tot(A)
2) Tot(R) & Tot(R) & Tot(R)
3) Tot(A) & Tot(R) & Tot(R)
4) Tot(A) & Tot(A) & Tot(R)
5) Tot(A) & Tot(A) & Cap(S)
6) Tot(A) & Tot(A) & Cap(A)
7) Tot(R) & Tot(R) & Cap(S)
8) Tot(R) & Tot(R) & Cap(A)
9) Tot(A) & Tot(R) & Cap(S)
10) Tot(A) & Tot(R) & Cap(A)
11) Tot(A) & Cap(A) & Cap(A)
12) Tot(A) & Cap(S) & Cap(S)
13) Tot(A) & Cap(S) & Cap(A)
14) Tot(R) & Cap(A) & Cap(A)
15) Tot(R) & Cap(S) & Cap(S)
16) Tot(R) & Cap(S) & Cap(A)

The Complete Constellation

1) Tot(A) & Tot(A) & Tot(A) & Tot(A) & Tot(A) & Tot(A)
2) Tot(A) & Tot(A) & Tot(A) & Tot(A) & Tot(A) & Tot(R)
3) Tot(A) & Tot(A) & Tot(A) & Tot(A) & Tot(R) & Tot(R)
4) Tot(R) & Tot(A) & Tot(A) & Tot(R) & Tot(R) & Tot(R)
5) Tot(A) & Tot(A) & Tot(R) & Tot(R) & Tot(R) & Tot(R)
6) Tot(A) & Tot(R) & Tot(R) & Tot(R) & Tot(R) & Tot(R)

```
7)  Tot(R) & Tot(R) & Tot(R) & Tot(R) & Tot(R) & Tot(R)
8)  Tot(A) & Tot(A) & Tot(A) & Tot(A) & Tot(A) & Cap(S)
9)  Tot(A) & Tot(A) & Tot(A) & Tot(A) & Cap(S) & Cap(S)
10) Tot(A) & Tot(A) & Tot(A) & Cap(S) & Cap(S) & Cap(S)
11) Tot(A) & Tot(A) & Cap(S) & Cap(S) & Cap(S) & Cap(S)
12) Tot(A) & Cap(S) & Cap(S) & Cap(S) & Cap(S) & Cap(S)
13) Tot(A) & Tot(A) & Tot(A) & Tot(A) & Tot(A) & Cap(A)
14) Tot(A) & Tot(A) & Tot(A) & Tot(A) & Cap(A) & Cap(A)
15) Tot(A) & Tot(A) & Tot(A) & Cap(A) & Cap(A) & Cap(A)
16) Tot(A) & Tot(A) & Cap(A) & Cap(A) & Cap(A) & Cap(A)
17) Tot(A) & Cap(A) & Cap(A) & Cap(A) & Cap(A) & Cap(A)
18) Tot(R) & Tot(R) & Tot(R) & Tot(R) & Tot(R) & Cap(S)
19) Tot(R) & Tot(R) & Tot(R) & Tot(R) & Cap(S) & Cap(S)
20) Tot(R) & Tot(R) & Tot(R) & Cap(S) & Cap(S) & Cap(S)
21) Tot(R) & Tot(R) & Cap(S) & Cap(S) & Cap(S) & Cap(S)
22) Tot(R) & Cap(S) & Cap(S) & Cap(S) & Cap(S) & Cap(S)
23) Tot(R) & Tot(R) & Tot(R) & Tot(R) & Tot(R) & Cap(A)
24) Tot(R) & Tot(R) & Tot(R) & Tot(R) & Cap(A) & Cap(A)
25) Tot(R) & Tot(R) & Tot(R) & Cap(A) & Cap(A) & Cap(A)
26) Tot(R) & Tot(R) & Cap(A) & Cap(A) & Cap(A) & Cap(A)
27) Tot(R) & Cap(A) & Cap(A) & Cap(A) & Cap(A) & Cap(A)
28) Tot(A) & Tot(A) & Tot(A) & Tot(A) & Tot(R) & Cap(S)
29) Tot(A) & Tot(A) & Tot(A) & Tot(R) & Tot(R) & Cap(S)
30) Tot(A) & Tot(A) & Tot(R) & Tot(R) & Tot(R) & Cap(S)
31) Tot(A) & Tot(R) & Tot(R) & Tot(R) & Tot(R) & Cap(S)
32) Tot(A) & Tot(A) & Tot(A) & Tot(A) & Tot(R) & Cap(A)
33) Tot(A) & Tot(A) & Tot(A) & Tot(R) & Tot(R) & Cap(A)
34) Tot(A) & Tot(A) & Tot(R) & Tot(R) & Tot(R) & Cap(A)
35) Tot(A) & Tot(R) & Tot(R) & Tot(R) & Tot(R) & Cap(A)
36) Tot(A) & Cap(S) & Cap(S) & Cap(S) & Cap(S) & Cap(A)
37) Tot(A) & Cap(S) & Cap(S) & Cap(S) & Cap(A) & Cap(A)
38) Tot(A) & Cap(S) & Cap(S) & Cap(A) & Cap(A) & Cap(A)
39) Tot(A) & Cap(S) & Cap(A) & Cap(A) & Cap(A) & Cap(A)
40) Tot(R) & Cap(S) & Cap(S) & Cap(S) & Cap(S) & Cap(A)
41) Tot(R) & Cap(S) & Cap(S) & Cap(S) & Cap(A) & Cap(A)
42) Tot(R) & Cap(S) & Cap(S) & Cap(A) & Cap(A) & Cap(A)
43) Tot(R) & Cap(S) & Cap(A) & Cap(A) & Cap(A) & Cap(A)
44) Tot(A) & Tot(R) & Cap(S) & Cap(S) & Cap(S) & Cap(A)
45) Tot(A) & Tot(R) & Cap(S) & Cap(S) & Cap(A) & Cap(A)
46) Tot(A) & Tot(R) & Cap(S) & Cap(A) & Cap(A) & Cap(A)
47) Tot(A) & Tot(A) & Tot(R) & Cap(S) & Cap(S) & Cap(A)
48) Tot(A) & Tot(A) & Tot(R) & Cap(S) & Cap(A) & Cap(A)
49) Tot(A) & Tot(A) & Tot(A) & Tot(R) & Cap(S) & Cap(A)
50) Tot(R) & Tot(R) & Tot(A) & Cap(S) & Cap(S) & Cap(A)
51) Tot(R) & Tot(R) & Tot(A) & Cap(S) & Cap(A) & Cap(A)
52) Tot(R) & Tot(R) & Tot(R) & Tot(A) & Cap(S) & Cap(A)
```

The same problems attend the investigation and illustration of reductionist constellations as complicate the identification and study of collaborative constellations. It seems, however, that evidence of reductionist relations is found more frequently than evidence of collaboration. Collaborative activity is precarious and difficult to sustain, while reductionist activity is relatively secure, self-assured, and more easily sustained. There does not exist, at the present time, a generally accepted intellectual integration of the variety of human endeavors which can provide the ballast for pursuits of the collaborative ideal. On the other hand, reductionist activity is stabilized by a more easily attainable knowledge of one set of horizon-specific ideals. While both collaborative and reductionist activity are mitigations of perplexity, the perplexity of the collaborative subject remains relatively severe.

The investigator seeking evidence of reductionist activity may be a collaborating, totalizing, or capitulating member of the complete constellation. If he is a collaborative member he may seek evidence of totalization and capitulation without a clear awareness of the influence of the ideal of differentiated unity upon his search, or he may apprehend annihilating and relegating totalization as mere criticism offered in a collaborative spirit and apprehend self-abandoning and subservient capitulation similarly as humble acknowledgements of the legitimacy and poignancy of the totalizer's 'critiques'. On the other hand, the collaborative student of culture may grasp too emphatically the genuine threat posed to his own horizonal integrity and autonomy by totalization and capitulation, and he may then turn from the investigative task to meet the apparently more pressing need to fight against reduction. Further, if the investigator is a totalizing and capitulating subject, his blindness to the over-reaching ideals of human subjectivity in general may lead to his misconception of totalization and capitulation as varieties of the superficial collaboration that is reasonable cooperation with an invader or aggressor.

The prior commitments which interfere with the task of the cultural investigator may also stand in the way of an understanding of the model being constructed. As the investigator seeking evidence of reductionist activity must hold in check his tendency to respond along the lines of his governing

92

ideal to the data he encounters, so one seeking to grasp the terms and relations of the model must appropriate a detached and disinterested stance and approach illustrations in that spirit. As interdisciplinary studies may illustrate imperfectly a variety of simple and complex collaborative constellations, so one may advert to the conflicts into which the various departments and faculties of universities enter and discover imperfect illustrations of reductionist constellations. However, a few, very general illustrations may facilitate an identification of reductionist activity. In The Revolt of the Masses Ortega y Gasset noted two troubling facts about his day.

First, the masses are to-day exercising functions in social life which coincide with those which hitherto seemed reserved to minorities; and secondly, these masses have at the same time shown themselves indocile to the minorities--they do not obey them, follow them, or respect them; on the contrary, they push them aside and supplant them.[14]

Ortega y Gasset is referring to the relationship of the ordinary horizon to the set of extraordinary horizons. He suggests that the ordinary horizon is totalizing in either an annihilating or a relegating fashion. It is not clear whether, in Ortega's view, the set of extraordinary horizons is capitulating in a self-abandoning or a subservient fashion, but there is the suggestion that ordinary totalization is meeting little resistance. Again, in The Betrayal of the Intellectuals Julien Benda describes a similar situation.

If I look at contemporary humanity from the point of view of its moral state as revealed in its political life, I see (a) A mass in whom realist passion in its two chief forms--class passion, national passion--has attained a degree of consciousness and organization hitherto unknown; (b) A body of men who used to be in opposition to the realism of the masses, but who now, not only do not oppose it, but adopt it, proclaim its grandeur and morality; in short, a humanity which has abandoned itself to realism with a unanimity, an absence of reserve, a sanctification of its passion unexampled in history.[15]

93

Benda speaks of the relationship of the ordinary horizon to the set of extraordinary horizons. The ordinary horizon, he suggests, is totalizing in an annihilating fashion. Moreover, he sees extraordinary subjects capitulating in a self-abandoning fashion.[16]

A review of reductionist permutations [See Chart 2] may aid the reader further in his personal pursuit of additional illustrations. For example, in a simple constellation, the religious horizon and the scientific horizon may both be totalizing in an annihilating fashion, or the scientific horizon may be totalizing in a relegating fashion and the religious horizon may be capitulating in a self-abandoning fashion. In a complex constellation with three member horizons the scientific horizon may be totalizing in a relegating fashion, the religious horizon may be capitulating in a self-abandoning fashion, and the philosophic horizon may be capitulating in a subservient fashion. Or, the philosophic horizon may be totalizing in a relegating fashion, and the artistic and scholarly horizons may be capitulating in a subservient fashion.[17]

2.3.3. HETEROGENEOUS CONSTELLATIONS

In an age lacking an adequate and generally accepted intellectual integration of human endeavors, the most common type of constellation is that in which both ideals are operative. Five types of activity are possible in a heterogeneous constellation: annihilating totalization [Tot(A)], relegating totalization [Tot(R)], self-abandoning capitulation [Cap(A)], subservient capitulation [Cap(S)], and resistance [Res]. Underlying heterogeneous forms are (i) reinforcements of original identifications, (ii) shifts of original identifications, and (iii) enforcements of the dissolution of original identifications. The internal perplexity that emerges with the actualization of a constellation is mitigated by efforts to totalize, capitulate, and resist.

A simple constellation in which both ideals are operative may take only two forms. Complex constellations with three member horizons may take nine forms. The complete constellation, with six member horizons, may take one hundred-and-five forms [See Chart 3]. In heterogeneous constellations there is always at least one totalizing horizon. Governance

94

CHART 3

CONSTELLATIONS GOVERNED BY MIXED IDEALS

Simple Constellations

1) Tot(A) & Res
2) Tot(R) & Res

Complex Constellations (3 Members)

1) Tot(A) & Tot(A) & Res
2) Tot(A) & Tot(R) & Res
3) Tot(R) & Tot(R) & Res
4) Tot(A) & Res & Res
5) Tot(R) & Res & Res
6) Tot(A) & Res & Cap(S)
7) Tot(A) & Res & Cap(A)
8) Tot(R) & Res & Cap(S)
9) Tot(R) & Res & Cap(A)

The Complete Constellation

1) Tot(A) & Tot(A) & Tot(A) & Tot(A) & Tot(A) & Res
2) Tot(A) & Tot(A) & Tot(A) & Tot(A) & Res & Res
3) Tot(A) & Tot(A) & Tot(A) & Res & Res & Res
4) Tot(A) & Tot(A) & Res & Res & Res & Res
5) Tot(A) & Res & Res & Res & Res & Res
6) Tot(R) & Tot(R) & Tot(R) & Tot(R) & Tot(R) & Res
7) Tot(R) & Tot(R) & Tot(R) & Tot(R) & Res & Res
8) Tot(R) & Tot(R) & Tot(R) & Res & Res & Res
9) Tot(R) & Tot(R) & Res & Res & Res & Res
10) Tot(R) & Res & Res & Res & Res & Res
11) Tot(A) & Tot(A) & Tot(A) & Tot(A) & Tot(R) & Res
12) Tot(A) & Tot(A) & Tot(A) & Tot(R) & Tot(R) & Res
13) Tot(A) & Tot(A) & Tot(R) & Tot(R) & Tot(R) & Res
14) Tot(A) & Tot(R) & Tot(R) & Tot(R) & Tot(R) & Res
15) Tot(A) & Tot(A) & Tot(A) & Tot(R) & Res & Res
16) Tot(A) & Tot(A) & Tot(R) & Tot(R) & Res & Res
17) Tot(A) & Tot(R) & Tot(R) & Tot(R) & Res & Res
18) Tot(A) & Tot(A) & Tot(R) & Res & Res & Res
19) Tot(A) & Tot(R) & Tot(R) & Res & Res & Res
20) Tot(A) & Tot(R) & Res & Res & Res & Res

21) Tot(A) & Tot(A) & Tot(A) & Tot(A) & Res & Cap(S)
22) Tot(A) & Tot(A) & Tot(A) & Res & Res & Cap(S)
23) Tot(A) & Tot(A) & Res & Res & Res & Cap(S)
24) Tot(A) & Res & Res & Res & Res & Cap(S)
25) Tot(R) & Tot(R) & Tot(R) & Tot(R) & Res & Cap(S)
26) Tot(R) & Tot(R) & Tot(R) & Res & Res & Cap(S)
27) Tot(R) & Tot(R) & Res & Res & Res & Cap(S)
28) Tot(R) & Res & Res & Res & Res & Cap(S)
29) Tot(A) & Tot(A) & Tot(A) & Tot(R) & Res & Cap(S)
30) Tot(A) & Tot(A) & Tot(R) & Tot(R) & Res & Cap(S)
31) Tot(A) & Tot(R) & Tot(R) & Tot(R) & Res & Cap(S)
32) Tot(A) & Tot(A) & Tot(R) & Res & Res & Cap(S)
33) Tot(A) & Tot(R) & Tot(R) & Res & Res & Cap(S)
34) Tot(A) & Tot(R) & Res & Res & Res & Cap(S)
35) Tot(A) & Tot(A) & Tot(A) & Tot(A) & Res & Cap(A)
36) Tot(A) & Tot(A) & Tot(A) & Res & Res & Res & Cap(A)
37) Tot(A) & Tot(A) & Res & Res & Res & Cap(A)
38) Tot(A) & Res & Res & Res & Res & Cap(A)
39) Tot(R) & Tot(R) & Tot(R) & Tot(R) & Res & Cap(A)
40) Tot(R) & Tot(R) & Tot(R) & Res & Res & Cap(A)
41) Tot(R) & Tot(R) & Res & Res & Res & Cap(A)
42) Tot(R) & Res & Res & Res & Res & Cap(A)
43) Tot(A) & Tot(A) & Tot(A) & Tot(R) & Res & Cap(A)
44) Tot(A) & Tot(A) & Tot(R) & Tot(R) & Res & Cap(A)
45) Tot(A) & Tot(R) & Tot(R) & Tot(R) & Res & Cap(A)
46) Tot(A) & Tot(A) & Tot(R) & Res & Res & Cap(A)
47) Tot(A) & Tot(R) & Tot(R) & Res & Res & Cap(A)
48) Tot(A) & Tot(R) & Res & Res & Res & Cap(A)
49) Tot(A) & Tot(A) & Tot(A) & Res & Cap(S) & Cap(S)
50) Tot(A) & Tot(A) & Res & Res & Cap(S) & Cap(S)
51) Tot(A) & Res & Res & Res & Cap(S) & Cap(S)
52) Tot(R) & Tot(R) & Tot(R) & Res & Cap(S) & Cap(S)
53) Tot(R) & Tot(R) & Res & Res & Cap(S) & Cap(S)
54) Tot(R) & Res & Res & Res & Cap(S) & Cap(S)
55) Tot(A) & Tot(A) & Tot(R) & Res & Cap(S) & Cap(S)
56) Tot(A) & Tot(R) & Tot(R) & Res & Cap(S) & Cap(S)
57) Tot(A) & Tot(R) & Res & REs & Cap(S) & Cap(S)
58) Tot(A) & Tot(A) & Res & Cap(S) & Cap(S) & Cap(S)
59) Tot(A) & Res & Res & Cap(S) & Cap(S) & Cap(S)
60) Tot(R) & Tot(R) & Res & Cap(S) & Cap(S) & Cap(S)
61) Tot(R) & Res & Res & Cap(S) & Cap(S) & Cap(S)
62) Tot(A) & Tot(R) & Res & Cap(S) & Cap(S) & Cap(S)
63) Tot(A) & Res & Cap(S) & Cap(S) & Cap(S) & Cap(S)
64) Tot(R) & Res & Cap(S) & Cap(S) & Cap(S) & Cap(S)
65) Tot(A) & Tot(A) & Tot(A) & Res & Cap(A) & Cap(A)
66) Tot(A) & Tot(A) & Res & Res & Cap(A) & Cap(A)
67) Tot(A) & Res & Res & Res & Cap(A) & Cap(A) & Cap(A)
68) Tot(R) & Tot(R) & Tot(R) & Res & Cap(A) & Cap(A)
69) Tot(R) & Tot(R) & Res & Res & Cap(A) & Cap(A)
70) Tot(R) & Res & Res & Res & Cap(A) & Cap(A)

71) Tot(A) & Tot(A) & Tot(R) & Res & Cap(A) & Cap(A)
72) Tot(A) & Tot(R) & Tot(R) & Res & Cap(A) & Cap(A)
73) Tot(A) & Tot(R) & Res & Res & Cap(A) & Cap(A)
74) Tot(A) & Tot(A) & Res & Cap(A) & Cap(A) & Cap(A)
75) Tot(A) & Res & Res & Cap(A) & Cap(A) & Cap(A)
76) Tot(R) & Tot(R) & Res & Cap(A) & Cap(A) & Cap(A)
77) Tot(R) & Res & Res & Cap(A) & Cap(A) & Cap(A)
78) Tot(A) & Tot(R) & Res & Cap(A) & Cap(A) & Cap(A)
79) Tot(A) & Res & Cap(A) & Cap(A) & Cap(A) & Cap(A)
80) Tot(R) & Res & Cap(A) & Cap(A) & Cap(A) & Cap(A)
81) Tot(A) & Tot(A) & Tot(A) & Res & Cap(S) & Cap(A)
82) Tot(A) & Tot(A) & Res & Res & Cap(S) & Cap(A)
83) Tot(A) & Res & Res & Res & Cap(S) & Cap(A)
84) Tot(R) & Tot(R) & Tot(R) & Res & Cap(S) & Cap(A)
85) Tot(R) & Tot(R) & Res & Res & Cap(S) & Cap(A)
86) Tot(R) & Res & Res & Res & Cap(S) & Cap(A)
87) Tot(A) & Tot(A) & Tot(R) & Res & Cap(S) & Cap(A)
88) Tot(A) & Tot(R) & Tot(R) & Res & Cap(S) & Cap(A)
89) Tot(A) & Tot(R) & Res & Res & Cap(S) & Cap(A)
90) Tot(A) & Tot(A) & Res & Cap(S) & Cap(S) & Cap(A)
91) Tot(A) & Res & Res & Cap(S) & Cap(S) & Cap(A)
92) Tot(R) & Tot(R) & Res & Cap(S) & Cap(S) & Cap(A)
93) Tot(R) & Res & Res & Cap(S) & Cap(S) & Cap(A)
94) Tot(A) & Tot(R) & Res & Cap(S) & Cap(S) & Cap(A)
95) Tot(A) & Res & Cap(S) & Cap(S) & Cap(S) & Cap(A)
96) Tot(R) & Res & Cap(S) & Cap(S) & Cap(S) & Cap(A)
97) tot(A) & Tot(A) & Res & Cap(S) & Cap(A) & Cap(A)
98) Tot(A) & Res & Res & Cap(S) & Cap(A) & Cap(A)
99) Tot(R) & Tot(R) & Res & Cap(S) & Cap(A) & Cap(A)
100) Tot(R) & Res & Res & Cap(S) & Cap(A) & Cap(A)
101) Tot(A) & Tot(R) & Res & Cap(S) & Cap(A) & Cap(A)
102) Tot(A) & Res & Cap(S) & Cap(A) & Cap(A) & Cap(A)
103) Tot(R) & Res & Cap(S) & Cap(A) & Cap(A) & Cap(A)
104) Tot(A) & Res & Cap(S) & Cap(S) & Cap(A) & Cap(A)
105) Tot(R) & Res & Cap(S) & Cap(S) & Cap(A) & Cap(A)

---

of intersubjective activity by the ideal of differentiated unity is exhibited by resistant activity. If there is also a capitulating member, then governance by the collaborative ideal is exhibited byresistance to both totalization and capitulation. If two or more resisting horizons combine in a complex heterogeneous constellation, they are related to one another as collaborating; resisting horizons do not resist one another's efforts of resistance.

Investigators seeking evidence of heterogeneous constellations face the same problems as those attempting to identify collaborative and reductionist activity. However, the significant activity in this case is the activity of resistance to totalization and capitulation. Investigators must hold in check their tendencies to respond to the data along the lines of their unexamined governing ideals of cultural unity. In that way they may preclude the misconception of resistant activity as mere recalcitrance or as critical activity with an ultimately reductionist aim. As prior commitments may interfere with the investigative task, so they may vitiate attempts to grasp the terms and relations of the model.

Earlier I directed attention to the works of Ortega y Gasset and Julien Benda in order to illustrate totalization and capitulation. But Ortega and Benda wrote the works cited in order to put a stop to ordinary totalization and extraordinary capitulation. Consequently, the two bodies of expression produced by these extraordinary subjects are themselves illustrations of resistance. Accordingly, Ortega and Benda direct their criticisms not only to "the masses" who are totalizing but also to les clercs (Benda) or "the minorities" (Ortega) who are capitulating. A resistant expression of the collaborative ideal is offered by Bellah in the same connection.

Perhaps America is too deeply committed to the active life in its pathological hypostatization to find again the healing balance of contemplation.[18]

Employing the fairly imprecise distinction between the vita activa and the vita contemplativa, Bellah laments extraordinary capitulation to ordinary totalization. Santayana resisted both ordinary and philosophic totalization.

Thus the many armed with prejudices and the few

armed with logic fight an eternal battle, the logical charging the physical world with unintelligibility and the man of common sense charging the logical world with abstractness and unreality . . . Each errs only in denouncing the other and wishing to be omnivorous, as if on the one hand logic could make anybody understand the history of events and the conjunction of objects, and on the other hand as if cognitive and moral processes could have any other terms than constant and ideal natures.[19]

Santayana's distinction between the physical world and the logical world may be inadequate, but his interest in preserving the autonomy and integrity of both horizons is evident. Carlyle took up the defense of the ordinary horizon against totalizing (natural) science. Of an eminent physiologist of his day he wrote:

We have the greatest admiration for this learned doctor: with what scientific stoicism he walks through the land of wonders, unwondering; like a wise man through some huge, gaudy Vauxhall, whose fireworks, cascades and symphonies, the vulgar may enjoy and believe in, --but where he finds nothing real but the saltpetre, pasteboard and catgut.[20]

But Carlyle was also sensitive to ordinary capitulation.

Sincere men, of never so limited intellect, have an instinct for discriminating sincerity. The cunningest Mephistopheles cannot deceive a single Margaret of honest heart; 'it stands written on his brow.' Masses of people capable of being led away by quacks are themselves of partially untrue spirit.[21]

The pursuit of additional illustrations may be facilitated by a review of heterogeneous permutations [See Chart 3]. For example, in a complex constellation with three member horizons the scientific and religious horizons may be totalizing, while the artistic horizon is resisting both totalizing movements. Or, the scientific horizon may be totalizing and five co-existing horizons may be resisting.[22]

2.3.4. INTERNAL HORIZONAL RELATIONS

Subjects sharing the same horizon may differ from one another as collaborating, resisting, capitulating, or totalizing. This additional complexity is exhibited by heterogeneous forms. Consider, for example, the three-member complex constellation:

[Tot(A) & Tot(R) & Res] & [Res & Cap(S) & Cap(A)] & [Cap(A) & Cap(S) & Res].

In constellations characterized by a great degree of internal horizonal differentiation, resistant subjects fight the totalizing and capitulating movements of other horizons and seek resistant unanimity in their own horizons. Totalizing subjects seek the capitulation of other horizons and totalizing unanimity in their own horizons. Capitulating subjects subjugate themselves to the totalizing horizons while seeking capitulating unanimity in their own horizons. Capitulating subjects do not capitulate to totalizing subjects sharing their horizons.

The three charts of permutations may be expanded to accommodate these additional variations arising from internal horizonal differences. It should be recalled, however, that these charts are based upon a consideration of only the basic range of intersubjective combinations of horizons [See Section 1.4.1. above]. The three charts, with the additional variations arising from internal horizonal differences, may be expanded by adverting to and symbolically representing the full range of possible combinations of horizons in single subjects. The resulting set of charts would constitute the symbolic representation of the complete model. It would represent a materially dynamic cultural matrix, and it could be employed as a model by the student of culture and the disorientated philosopher seeking to ascertain his responsible cultural role.

NOTES TO CHAPTER III

[1] This is not to say that there were no signs of artistic, philosophic, scientific, and scholarly modes of operation. See,

for examples, B. Snell, The Discovery of the Mind. See also
Daniel Guerriere, "The Structure of Mythic Existence," The Personalist (Summer, 1974), 263-264: "All those dimensions of experience called art, play, sexuality, politics, economics, medi-
cine, religion, and so on—which we live in a discontinuous
fashion—form, for compact man, a compact whole. For example,
sowing seed or trapping the boar is as much a religious and
political praxis as an economic one. Sexuality is artistic,
political, playful, economic, and religious at once. War is
play and politics and religion. Simply trying to understand
the world is a literary, philosophical, scientific, religious,
and political act; ancient astronomy, for example, is all of
these. Every polis is a theocracy. A meal is economics, play,
and religion at once." The self-present subject plucks out,
as it were, each aspiration from the ordinary mixture or blend
of aspirations. The ordinary subject, for example, remembers;
but it is the artistic subject who undertakes to make things
and events memorable. Again, the ordinary subject inquires,
wonders, asks questions; but it is the emerging philosophic
subject who commands himself, in the person of Parmenides' Goddess, Inquire into everything. Again, it is commonly held that
philosophy emerged during the period from 800 to 200 B.C. The
series of events which took place have been characterized in
a variety of ways: the Axial Age (K. Jaspers); the discovery
of mind (B. Snell); the leap into being (E. Voegelin); the pri-
mordial revelation of Being as Being (M. Heidegger); the shift
or transition from undifferentiated to theoretically differentiated consciousness (B. Lonergan); the philosophic breakthrough
(T. Parsons). Prior to the emergence of the philosophic horizon,
there were ordinary, artistic, and religious subjects. Ordinary
and religious subjects existed long before the poets, and the
poets existed long before the emergence of philosophers. In
the absence of philosophers, the poets had played the roles
of prophet and sage. This arrogation of what was to become a
strictly philosophic function constitutes evidence in support
of the view, expressed by E. Voegelin and shared by Lonergan,
that the history of conscious intentionality may be a development
from compact to differentiated consciousness. See Voegelin's
Order and History, Vol. IV: The Ecumenic Age (Baton Rouge: Louisiana State University Press, 1974), Introduction; also, Lonergan, Method in Theology, the Index under "differentiations of
consciousness". The notion of differentiation is significant
inasmuch as it provides a tentative answer to the question,
Where do horizons come from?

[2] On intersubjectivity, art, symbols, languages, and lives
and deeds of persons as carriers of meaning, see Lonergan, Method
in Theology, Chap. 3.

[3] It may be objected that to venture beyond a consideration

of the relations of mutually physically-present subjects to one another renders the tasks of the student of culture and the philosopher excessively complex. Even the preparatory task requires advertence to the existing cultural matrix, and so it too is complicated by the broad notion of presence. Wouldn't these tasks be completed more easily if a control group were convened and closely observed? A thought-experiment will reveal the deficiencies of this manner of proceeding.

Let us imagine a round-table discussion on the future of human endeavor in Western culture. To meet our requirements, this meeting would have to represent in microcosm the complete constellation. It will be attended, then, by representatives of the full range of human endeavors constitutive of our culture: one ordinary subject, one artistic subject, one scientific subject, one scholarly subject, one philosophic subject, and one religious subject. We must be willing to settle for a group composed of one ordinary subject and the variety of basic combinations, for each a truly representative group would be too large. Let us imagine now that each participant states his case in his own manner, according to his horizonal lights. The constellation, which was merely potential at the start, will quickly become actual; horizonal dissonance will become apparent even thought the differences may not be immediately specifiable. We may now imagine the group members to call a temporary halt to the proceedings. All of the participants are at least commonsensical; all recognize the impracticality of continuing in the same manner. Discussion of the topic which brought the members together is postponed in favor of the pursuit of agreement on how to proceed. All agree that nothing will be accomplished if each continues to operate in his own manner and express himself in his own way. The point to the meeting, they all agree, is to get something done, to come to some type of agreement on measures to be taken to preserve their culture. The alternatives are reviewed. Each participant could learn to operate and express himself in the manners of the others. But this, it is commonly recognized, would require an enormous general effort of learning which time will not permit. On the other hand, it is pointed out that one in the group can already be understood by all of the others. An agreement is reached; all will restrict themselves to ordinary language and employ only those words and phrases which everyone can understand. The extraordinary participants agree to avoid using their peculiar technical languages and idioms, and to abandon for the time being their peculiar modes of operation.

Let us now reflect on what has taken place in this round-table discussion. To prevent the dissolution of the meeting in a highly impractical anarchy, the commonsense mode of operation and expression has been given a dominant position. In effect, measures have been taken to reduce an actual constellation to a mere collection of commonsense subjects, a potential constellation. The topic at hand, which originally mediated a common recognition of horizonal dissonance, is intentionally bounded by self-imposed restrictions; it is defined beforehand as a topic that cannot bear extraordinary treatment. The relationships that emerge among the participants cannot be taken as representative of the relationships characteristic of the entire cultural matrix. In virtue of the mutual physical presence of the subjects, the range of response is artificially limited. It may happen to be true that the capitulation of extraordinary subjects to the ordinary horizon is characteristic of the cultural matrix into which the observers are inquiring. But, because the subjects are physically present to one another, the experiment is inadequately controlled and the observer cannot conclude objectively that the culture as a whole is similarly constituted. Moreover, for the same reason, the meeting does not provide sufficient data for the preparatory determination of the range of possible relations between horizons. In mutual physical presence, the ordinary horizon which all subjects share exerts an inertial influence. In the interest of getting things done, mutual understanding is preferred to mutual incomprehension, and the full range of actually possible cultural relations is not given an opportunity to emerge.

[4] R. G. Collingwood noted the same phenomenon: "Every person who is actually absorbed in any given form of experience is by this very absorption committed to the opinion that no other form is valid, that his form is the only one adequate to the comprehension of reality . . .. When artists and scientists, who after all do inhabit a common world of fact, meet and discuss their aims, each is apt to accuse the other of wasting his life on a worlds of illusions." See Speculum Mentis, p. 307.

[5] The notion of basic horizon employed here is not merely the product of a Kantian-type deduction of abstract conditions of the possibility of horizonal perplexity. While it is true that horizonal perplexity could not arise if a distinction were not drawn, however vaguely and inadequately, between horizon-specific ideals and ideals of subjectivity in general, it seems also to be the case that horizonal conflict does in fact hinge on the employment of the distinction. So what is at issue here is not the existence or non-existence of a basic horizon, but the fact that the presupposition of its existence is commonly maintained. I am, therefore, applying a methodological principle similar to the Thomas Theorem in sociology: if men define situations as real, they are real in their consequences. Schutz has rephrased the principle: if an appresentational relationship is socially approved, then the appresented object, fact, or event is believed beyond question, even if fictional, to be in its typicality an element in the world taken for granted. See Schutz's Collected Papers I: The Problem of Social Reality,

ed. Maurice Natanson (The Hague: Martinus Nijhoff, 1962), pp. 294 ff. and p. 303. However, there are also good grounds for assuming that a basic horizon could be discovered by investigating the worlds of the variety of horizons in their self-present dimensions, that is, as modes of operation and standpoints. The discovery of this basic horizon would not be a grasp of being in its totality; but it would constitute a heuristic grasp of it. The assumption or presupposition of common subjective ideals is seemingly incorrigible and ineradicable: even subjects who identify their horizon-specific ideals with the only adequate ideals defend their identifications and so exhibit a faith in a deep mode which might enable those with different horizons to be convinced. In brief, to deny the distinction between horizon-specific ideals and ideals of human subjectivity in general is to rely upon the distinction, just as the sceptic's defense of his position is an undermining of his position. So it is that accounts of the deep mode of operation are normally accompanied by the claim that critics of the accounts undo themselves by performatively confirming the accounts. See, for example, Lonergan, Insight, Chap. XI, and Method in Theology, p. 17.

⁶ Georg Simmel, Conflict & The Web of Group-Affiliations, trans. Kurt H. Wolff and Reinhard Bendix (New York: The Free Press, 1955), p. 17.

⁷ The distinction between annihilating and relegating totalization is employed, in different language, by Otto A. Bird, Cultures in Conflict, pp. 5, 51, 178-184.

⁸ Totalizing movements have been recognized in other contexts. Bacon employed the notion, in different terms, in connection with impediments to the advance of the sciences. He is quoted by Newman, who brought the same notion to bear in his defense of theology as a branch of knowledge against what he perceived to be an invasion by the natural sciences of co-existing disciplines: "Men have used to infect their meditations, opinions, and doctrines, with some conceits which they have most admired, or some Sciences which they have most applied; and give all things else a tincture according to them utterly untrue and improper . . .. So have the alchemists made a philosophy out of a few experiments of the furnace; and Gilbertus, our countryman, hath made a philosophy out of the observations of a lodestone. So Cicero, when, reciting the several opinions of the nature of the soul, he found a musician that held the soul was but a harmony, saith pleasantly, 'Hic ab arte sua non recessit [He was true to his art].' But of these conceits Aristotle speaketh seriously and wisely when he saith, 'Qui respiciunt ad pauca, de facili pronunciant [They who contemplate a few things have no difficulty in deciding].'" See Newman's The Idea of a University, p. 109. More recently, Konrad Lorenz has observed the

104

tendency of innovative thinkers to overstate the significance of their discoveries. He finds such overstatement in connection with Loeb's discovery of the principle of tropisms, Pavlov's discovery of the conditioned reflex, and Freud's invention of psychoanalysis. See his Preface to Charles Darwin, The Expression of the Emotions in Man and Animals (Chicago, London: The University of Chicago Press, 1965), ix. Perhaps the clearest illustration of a totalizing movement is that which follows rapidly upon a political revolution. The installation of a new regime is normally succeeded by a deliberate subjugation or purge of the opposition.

[9] By a detached and disinterested view or stance is meant one dominated by interests or anticipations or a particular type, rather than a stance free of interests and anticipations. An illustration of the degree of involvement characteristic of scientific 'detachment' is provided by Lonergan, Insight, pp. 73-74. The detachment of which I speak is analogous to natural scientific detachment; while it does not require a restriction to sensible data, it does require a dominance of conscious intentionality by a desire or interest to understand correctly.

[10] See Otto Bird, Cultures in Conflict, Chap. 8, pp. 137-153.

[11] J. H. Newman, The Idea of a University, p. 133.

[12] Jacques Barzun, The House of Intellect (New York: Harper, 1959), pp. 145-146. The philosophico-religious movement of Transcendentalism may have tipped the balance toward ordinary dominance. The suggestion is made and amply illustrated by Richard Hofstadter in Anti-Intellectualism in American Life (New York: Vintage Books, 1962), p. 70. See also, Morton White, Science and Sentiment in America (New York: Oxford University Press, 1972) and "Reflections on Anti-Intellectualism," Daedalus, Vol. 91 (1962), 457-468.

[13] The notion of reduction employed throughout this chapter and the next is not the same as the notion commonly encountered in articles and books on issues in philosophy of science. The reductionist trend discussed by philosophers of science is characterized by a series of capitulations; it is a re-compacting of a telescoped hierarchy of sciences. See, for example, the account of the reductionist trend given by Barry Commoner in The Closing Circle (New York: Alfred A. Knopf, 1971), p. 191: "It often leads sociologists to become psychologists, psychologists to become physiologists, physiologists to become cellular biologists, and turns cellular biologists into chemists, chemists into physicists, and physicists into mathematicians." This notion is similar to the one employed in the present chapter, for both

imply a re-compacting. However, this notion pertains to a re-compacting of sciences, while my notion implies a re-compacting of horizons.

[14] Jose Ortega y Gasset, The Revolt of the Masses, trans. Anon. (London: Unwin Books, 1961), p. 17.

[15] Julien Benda, The Betrayal of the Intellectuals, p. 143.

[16] For another detailed account of extraordinary capitulation to ordinary totalization, see Thomas Molnar, The Decline of the Intellectual (New York: Meridian Books, 1961). Note that Benda's objectification of the situation relies upon a verbal context which is partially capitulatory. His employments of 'realist' and 'realism' reflect the inadequacy of his own analysis of ordinary totalization; for it is a totalizing ordinary horizon which claims to be the realist horizon. Insofar as Benda surrenders the notion of reality to the ordinary horizon, he diminishes also his ability to defend his claims of integrity and autonomy for extraordinary subjects; for he must rely upon the inherently weaker notion of 'idealism' in his defense.

[17] Consider, for example, "the old quarrel between philosophy and poetry" mentioned by Plato [Republic 607b]. Earlier, Heraclitus had attacked Hesiod as a rival authority [Fr. 57], describing him as learned certainly, but lacking in intelligence [Frs. 40, 42]. And Plato, although he gave beauty a crucial role in his philosophic writings, practically defined it so as to exclude art. Iris Murdoch's short work, The Fire and the Sun, Why Plato Banished the Artists (New York: Oxford University Press, 1978), is a good source for an understanding of Plato's ambivalent relationship to the artistic horizon. Plato's banishment of some types of artist from the ideal Republic, and his suggestion that art is fundamentally frivolous, have troubled artists and scholars for centuries. See his remarks in Republic 398a-c and 595 ff. Incidentally, scholars, those who reflected upon art and evaluated it, fared almost as badly. "Arguments about poetry," said Plato, "remind me of provincial drinking parties" [Protagoras 347c]. The ordinary horizon also had its status in the existing constellation reduced. Plato's allegory of the cave is the lasting representation of the difference between the ordinary horizon and the philosophic [Republic 514a]. The cave allegory depicts two distinct standpoints (those of the lover of wisdom and the lover of opinion), two distinct modes of operation (the scientific faculty and the opining faculty), and two distinct worlds (the intelligible world and the visible world) [Republic 475c-476d, 480; 477a-478a]. Earlier, Parmenides had warned, through the Goddess: Avoid the way ruled by the eye; and Heraclitus had asserted that the majority of mankind are "unaware of what they are doing after they wake"

[Fr. 1]. The totalizing movement characteristic of emergent philosophy is carried by Plato to its limit. The inferior status of the horizon of the multitude is explicitly affirmed. Neither the lover of opinion nor the lover of sights and sounds attains truth. Moreover, neither sees "the last thing to be seen" in the upper region of the intelligibles, the idea of the Good [Republic 517a-d]. But, Plato says, "Anyone who is to act wisely in private or public life must have caught sight of this." In the ideal Republic the guardianship of the city is to be undertaken by those who have most understanding of principles, and it is the philosopher alone who has this understanding [Republic 521b]. While Plato attempts to avoid an absolute condemnation of the multitude, inasmuch as he claims that ordinary subjects are capable of distinguishing the sophist from the true philosopher [Republic 499e-500], it remains that his position constitutes a reductionist integration of human endeavors. The philosopher may succeed in convincing the multitude of his difference from the sophists whom ordinary subjects despise, but he is then faced with the difficult task of convincing the multitude that he alone has access to being and the good. The perplexity felt by ordinary subjects before the prospect of being led by sophists is ultimately deepened by internal horizonal perplexity before this totalizing philosophic claim. Prudent deference to philosophers is one thing, but a total relinquishment of horizonal integrity and autonomy is quite another.

Religious totalization may be illustrated by some Christian Fathers' attacks on secular learning. The text and symbol for religious denunciations of the pride of intellect was often the philosopher Plato. "All the assertions of the philosophers about the eternity of the world and the ideas, and that soul of the world that they call noys are utterly destroyed and confounded by the first chapter of Genesis." Again: "How much more estimable the philosophy that does not discourse idly of the stars and the nature of things in the style of Plato, but treats humbly and usefully of the correction of morals and the practice of virtues." [These expressions are quoted by Paul Shorey, Platonism Ancient and Modern (Berkeley: University of California Press, 1938), pp. 82-83] The horizon-relative character of the first expression is evident. Only insofar as the philosopher shares the religious subject's apprehension of Genesis is he likely to be confounded or even slightly troubled by its account of the origin of the cosmos. Again, only a religious subject who overlooks horizonal differences completely could expect such an expression to give a philosopher pause. The second expression is especially striking, however, in view of Plato's love of the Good. From a philosophic standpoint, ignorance of this keystone of Platonic thought is almost beyond belief. Nevertheless, when one takes into account the fact that the reduction of the status of any horizon normally involves the wholesale "writing off" of its self-expression by the total-

107

izing subject, this enormous oversight, while still disturbing, appears to be consistent.

Religious totalization may be illustrated further by the Inquisition. However, the Inquisition is often cited to expose the dangers of religious domination. It should be noted that to appeal to the Inquisition to illustrate religious totalization is not to make as well a negative judgment on the significance or adequacy or legitimacy of the religious horizon as such. Allusions to the Inquisition are often at root condemnations of the religious horizon itself; as such, they are simply further illustrations of totalizing activity. There may be as many 'inquisitions' as there are horizons capable of totalizing themselves and subsequently gaining socio-political hegemony.

Numerous illustrations of ordinary totalization may be found in Richard Hofstadter's Anti-Intellectualism in American Life.

For a discussion of (natural) scientific totalization and capitulating artists, scholars and philosophers, see Leo Marx, "Reflections on the Neo-Romantic Critique of Science," Daedalus (Spring, 1978). See also Freud's totalizing expression in New Introductory Lectures on Psychoanalysis, trans. James Strachey (Harmondsworth: Penguin Books, 1973), pp. 195-196, 207-208; also, The Future of an Illusion, trans. W. D. Robson-Scott (New York: Anchor Books, 1964), pp. 62-63, 92. See also, Jean Piaget on philosophy in Insights and Illusions of Philosophy, trans. Wolfe Mays (New York: The World Publishing Company, 1971), pp. 121 and 216.

For illuminating discussions, with illustrations, of artistic capitulation to scientific totalization and of artistic totalization, see A. W. Raitt, Life and Letters in France, The Nineteenth Century (New York: Scribner's, 1965), xxvi, pp. 29, 69, 93-95, 98, 99, 104, 106.

C. P. Snow's The Two Cultures and the Scientific Revolution (Cambridge: Cambridge University Press, 1959) explores the relationship of scientific to literary intellectuals. Snow, a scientific and artistic subject, favors science and consequently apprehends an "unqualified hostility to science" among artists. See Leo Marx, Ibid., 66, and Herbert Read, To Hell with Culture (New York: Schocken Books, 1964), pp. 178 ff., especially p. 179.

The capitulation of scholarly subects to scientific totalization is revealed in I. A. Richards' early works, Principles of Literary Criticism and Science and Poetry. In these works Richards advocates the scholarly emulation of "scientific objectivity". This view had a long afterlife within the movement of "new criticism" (1930-1960). Even though proponents of "new criticism" were occasionally antagonistic toward science, Leo Marx argues that they nevertheless emulated the scientific mode of operation. See Leo Marx, Ibid., 66-67.

[18]Robert N. Bellah, "To Kill and Survive or To Die and Become: The Active Life and the Contemplative Life as Ways of Being Adult," _Daedalus_ (Spring 1976), 73-74.

[19]_The Life of Reason_, Vol. I, _Reason in Common Sense_ (New York: Collier Books, 1962), p. 122.

[20]_Thomas Carlyle: Selected Writings_, ed. Alan Shelston (Harmondsworth: Penguin Books, 1971), p. 69.

[21]_Ibid._, pp. 182-183.

[22]G. K. Chesterton resisted the totalizing activity of extraordinary subjects. "Thus far my thesis is this: that it is not the Uncommon Man who is persecuted but rather the Common Man. But this brings me into direct conflict with the contemporary reaction, which seems to say, in effect, that the Common Man had much better be persecuted. It is quite certain that many modern thinkers and writers honestly feel a contempt for the Common Man; it is also quite certain that I myself feel a contempt for those who feel this contempt." See _The Common Man_ (London: Sheed and Ward, 1950), p. 6.

Francisco Goya had the advantage of powerful protectors during the Inquisition, so he was not molested. Nevertheless, he did express resistance to religious totalization in defense of others less fortunate. "Painting, like poetry, selects in the universe whatever she deems most appropriate to her ends. She assembles in a single fantastic personage circumstances and features which nature distributes among many individuals. From this combination, ingeniously composed, results that happy imitation by virtue of which the artist earns the title of inventor and not of servile copyist." Goya was objecting to the imposition of the standards of propriety, fitness, and suitability of religious subjects upon the artist. See _Artists on Art_, eds. Marco Treves and Robert Goldwater (New York: Pantheon Books, 1958), pp. 203-204. See also the revealing transcript of Paolo Caliari Veronese's inquisition, in which the conflict of standards of propriety is clearly illustrated, on pp. 104-108.

Freud has himself provided an illustration of religious resistance to scientific totalization. See his _New Introductory Lectures_, pp. 208-209.

The interested reader may find in Otto Bird's work, _Cultures in Conflict_, studies of a variety of conflicts which, I believe, are rooted in horizonal differences.

IV

PHILOSOPHY'S PLACE IN CULTURE: A PROSPECTUS

In Chapter I I outlined the general form of
the horizonal structure. In Chapter III I augmented
the outline with an account of the types of dynamic
relationships into which co-existing horizons may
enter. The expanded model constitutes a way of approaching determinate answers to the following questions: (i) What is the present cultural situation?
(ii) What task may philosophers reasonably be called
upon to perform in our culture? The first question,
if it is raised in a scientific manner, is the leading
question of the student of culture, and it may be
broken down, as it were, into two questions: (a)
What is the present cultural situation? (b) What
was the cultural situation in the past? Now, the
manner in which the model might inform cultural investigations could be investigated at length; but
the aim of the present essay requires that the model
be related to the process of answering question (ii),
the leading question of the disorientated philosopher.
The answer to this question depends in part upon
answers to the two types of question raised by the
student of culture; a knowledge of the demands of
the present depends upon a knowledge of the present
situation, and a knowledge of the present situation
depends in part upon a knowledge of previous cultural
situations. However, my aim in the present chapter
is to employ the horizonal structure to describe
generally the process from cultural disorientation
to deliberate philosophic engagement in a culture.
Accordingly, the emphasis in my discussion falls,
not on the methodical procedures of sociology and
anthropology and cultural history, but on the self-
orientating procedures of the philosopher.

The point to this additional exposition, it
should be noted, is not to provide a determinate

answer to the leading question of the disorientated philosopher. The upcoming exposition constitutes an extension of the model in the specific direction of an answer which each philosopher must obtain for himself. Decisions affecting the course of one's cultural involvement, as recent existentialist reflections have shown, do not simply follow logically from the arguments of others. The present chapter is the final stage of a preparatory maneuver. Accordingly, in the first section I shall review the options facing the disorientated philosopher; in the second section I shall present a model of the process of deliberation by which philosophic subjects may orientate themselves; in the third section I shall illustrate the use of the deliberative model by placing the results of my own deliberations within its structure; in a final section I shall explore briefly a notion of philosophic engagement which emerges from the personal illustration.

1. OPTIONS

In Chapter III two guiding ideals of cultural unity were distinguished, the reductionist ideal and the ideal of differentiated unity. According to the model, the philosopher concerned to orientate himself in his culture may choose to pursue the reductionist ideal or the collaborative ideal. By choosing to pursue the reductionist ideal, the philosopher commits himself to one of the following types of activity in relation to co-existing horizons: annihilating totalization [Tot(A)]; relegating totalization [Tot(R)]; self-abandoning capitulation [Cap(A)]; subservient capitulation [Cap(S)]. On the other hand, by choosing to pursue the collaborative ideal, the philosopher commits himself to collaboration [Col] or resistance [Res].

The disorientated philosopher, then, is faced with two major options, according to the model. Depending upon his choice of a cultural ideal, he is faced with either two or four minor options. However, it may happen that the philosopher does not experience cultural disorientation, that he does not see the need for deliberate reflection on these options. According to the model, his indifference may have several causes. First, the philosopher may have gone through the deliberative process of self-orientation previously. Second, the philosopher may not have been a member of an actual constellation.

If the philosopher has already gone through the deliberative process of self-orientation, he has already committed himself to participation in his constellation under the governance of either the reductionist or the collaborative ideal. His cultural activity is deliberate or premeditated. However, a repetition of the deliberative process with the aid of the horizonal structure still has worth in that it provides an occasion for a deepening of the philosopher's self-understanding and his under-standing of his cultural milieu.

If the philosopher has not been a member of an actual constellation, he may be participating in his culture while still remaining relatively iso-lated from subjects of other horizons. His participa-tion, then, may be governed by the ideal of cultural unity subscribed to by "normal philosophy". Inasmuch as his cultural activity is grounded upon another's deliberate or unpremeditated resolution of internal horizonal perplexity, it is unpremeditated and so also worthy of suspicion. The deliberative process of self-orientation remains to be gone through.

Cultural participation cannot be avoided except by maintaining complete isolation. But complete iso-lation also prevents the emergence of a horizon. If one is exercising common sense or practicing art, science, scholarship, philosophy, or religion, one has chosen, either deliberately or without premedi-tation, an ideal of cultural unity. Because commit-ment is inevitable if one has a horizon, the wise or merely rational course to follow, if the experience of disorientation is absent, is the course of deliber-ate self-orientation. If one's disorientation has already been legitimately eliminated, a repetition of the deliberative process with the aid of a new model of culture will further strengthen conviction and commitment. On the other hand, if one's conviction and commitment have never been questioned, the de-liberative process may provide the self-understanding and cultural understanding that lead to either the correction of one's orientation or its solidification in methodical activity.

Finally, it may happen that the philosopher experiences cultural disorientation but chooses, for whatever reason, to ignore it. In this case the philosopher has suppressed the problem of orientation posed by horizonal dissonance and multiplicity, and he has arrested the deliberative process motivated by internal perplexity. It remains, however, that he participates in his culture, that he does in fact take a stand by his actions, that by refusing to choose he nonetheless makes a choice. His refusal to orientate himself deliberately is in fact an expression of his preference for incomplete deliberation.

1.1. SPONTANEOUS AND DELIBERATE ACTIVITY

Each of the six minor options confronting the philosopher may be exercised spontaneously or deliberately. Totalization, capitulation, collaboration, and resistance may be spontaneous, habitual, unpremeditated. As potential constellations become actual, the adequacy of particular horizons is called into question. Horizonal dissonance promotes a temporary suspension, as it were, of previous involvement. In this interval, two types of accommodation of internal perplexity may take place. On the one hand, perplexity may be <u>immediately accommodated</u>; on the other, it may be <u>deliberately accommodated</u>. By immediate accommodation is meant either the simple reinstitution of previous involvement without deliberation or the institution of essentially similar involvement without deliberation. By deliberate accommodation is meant the completion of a deliberative process and the subsequent institution of a type of involvement that has been found to be worthwhile.

Immediate accommodation is the reinstitution of previous involvement without benefit of deliberation or the institution of essentially similar involvement without benefit of deliberation. First, if previous involvement was governed by the reductionist ideal, immediate accommodation may take the form of a renewal of the natural identification, typical of incipient horizons, of horizon-specific ideals with the ideals of human subjectivity in general. On the other hand, it may take the form of a transformation of the natural identification and a shift to capitulating allegiance to a co-existing totalizing horizon. However, the accommodating horizon may be relatively mature, and its previous involvement may have been totalizing or capitulating. In such cases, immediate accommodation takes the form of a simple reinstitution of previous involvement. Second,

114

if previous involvement was governed by the ideal of differentiated unity, immediate accommodation may take the form of a simple reinstitution of previous collaborative or resistant activity. Immediate accommodation, clearly, does not bring about an essential change in a constellation.

Deliberate accommodation is the completion of a deliberative process and the subsequent institution of a type of involvement that has been found to be worthwhile. It is a meditative response to the motivation of horizonal perplexity rather than an unpremeditated reversion or inessential transformation. Deliberate accommodation requires of the philosopher that he abide in the state of suspension, that he advert to the tension of that state, and that he employ his experience of the tension as evidence to support the judgment that serious deliberation is indeed required. The tension of disengagement is the very spontaneity that calls for reflection; it is the tension created by the inhibition of habitual routines. Deliberate accommodation may terminate in totalization, capitulation, collaboration, or resistance; however, these activities are now deliberate instead of spontaneous. The mere experience of oneself as participating in one's culture has been augmented by an identification of the type of participation and the ideal by which it is governed; moreover, one's participation may be essentially transformed as a consequence of one's deliberative reflection on its value. In the end, one settles on an ideal of unity and one becomes methodical in the pursuit of it, proceeding according to a fairly well-ordered plan; one's pursuit is neither wholly spontaneous nor dilatory. Deliberate accommodation brings about an essential change in a constellation.

The distinction between spontaneous and deliberate activity introduces into the horizonal structure an additional determination. Each of the three types of horizonal constellations may be spontaneous, semideliberate, or deliberate. A spontaneous constellation is one in which all of the member subjects have immediately accommodated horizonal perplexity. A deliberate constellation is one in which all of the member subjects have deliberately accommodated their perplexity. A semideliberate constellation is one in which subjects of one or more, but not all, member horizons have deliberately accommodated horizonal perplexity.

2. THE PROCESS OF SELF-ORIENTATION

The process of deliberation by which we orientate ourselves is, most generally, a set of sequentially-ordered operations terminating in decisive action. Ordinary, artistic, scholarly, philosophic, scientific, and religious subjects deliberate; all are called upon, with greater or less frequency, to make decisions. Accordingly, to speak of a deliberative process is to allude to what has been named the deep mode of conscious and intentional operations [See Chapter I, Section 6]. The extension of the horizonal structure in the direction of philosophic self-orientation, then, requires at least a general reference to the deep mode. In particular, it requires a reference to a specific set of operations occurring in a specific sequence. To give my exposition of the deliberative process of self-orientation a structure, I shall make use of Bernard Lonergan's account of deliberative operations.

In his attempt to provide an account of the deep mode informing every horizon-specific mode, Lonergan has distinguished four levels of conscious and intentional operation: (i) the empirical level of seeing, hearing, touching, tasting, smelling, anticipating, remembering, and imagining; (ii) the intellectual level of questioning, understanding, conceiving, formulating, and hypothesizing; (iii) the rational level of reflective questioning, weighing the evidence, grasping the fulfilment of the conditions for a judgment, and judging; and (iv) the level of responsibility on which, Lonergan writes,

> we are concerned with ourselves, with our operations, our goals, and so deliberate about possible courses of action, evaluate them, decide, and carry out our decisions.[1]

In order to provide a structure for my exposition of the process of philosophic self-orientation, I shall employ the sequentially-ordered set of operations -- deliberation, evaluation, decision.

Several characteristics of Lonergan's account of deliberative operations and their sequence recommend it for use in the present context. First, Lonergan employs the terms 'deliberate', 'evaluate', and 'decide' in their familiar, ordinary senses. Consequently, the exposition is not complicated by the

116

requirement that one have a technical grasp of the nature of deliberative or responsible consciousness; all that is required is an ability to identify the operations in one's own conscious experience in the manner of the ordinary subject. Second, Lonergan's account is very general, first, because his intention is to expose the deep mode of operation and, second, because his account is explicitly designed to 'save' every horizon-specific mode of operation that has emerged so far.[2] Again, Lonergan's account of the deep mode is not merely a contribution to the unification of the various natural sciences, or the various human or social sciences; nor is it merely a contribution to the integration of science and religion. Rather, Lonergan's account is offered for the purpose of unifying methodologically the standpoints, worlds, and modes of operation of ordinary, artistic, scientific, scholarly, philosophic, and religious subjects. Consequently, Lonergan's account of deliberative operations provides a capacious frame for the extension of the horizonal structure in the direction not only of philosophic self-orientation but also in the directions of ordinary, scientific, artistic, scholarly, and religious self-orientation. The employment of Lonergan's account of deliberation to facilitate the extension of the horizonal structure in this specific case does not close off the possibility of additional analogous extensions. However, my present concern is to bring the horizonal structure to bear upon the process of philosophic self-orientation.

2.1. DELIBERATION: REFLECTIVE DISENGAGEMENT

The process of self-orientation begins with reflective disengagement from active cultural involvement. When I begin to question my involvement I withdraw from philosophic activity; I am no longer producing philosophic works or having philosophic discussions. Naturally, I do not shed my cultural context as a snake sheds its skin; rather, the reflective disengagement with which the process begins, is the exploitation of a given capacity to take stock of myself and my involvement. But there is always the danger, subsequent to the emergence of internal horizonal perplexity, of immediate accommodation. Accordingly, reflective disengagement may be promoted by raising and attempting to answer two questions. First, what is the present situation? Second, how do I stand

in the present situation? Since reflective disengagement constitutes the initial phase of the process
of deliberation, these two questions must be raised
in the context of an intention to answer eventually
a third: How should I stand in the present situation?
The horizonal structure may be employed now as a
heuristic device.

What type of constellation exists? Three types
of constellation are possible subsequent to the emergence of a multiplicity of horizons: reductionist,
collaborative, and heterogeneous. What is the trend
of my constellation? Is one horizon dominant? If
so, is its dominance a function of totalization and
capitulation? Are all horizons collaborating? Are
some horizons resisting while others are totalizing?
On the basis afforded by the horizonal structure,
a set of questions relevant to the identification
of one's situation may be generated.

How do I stand in the existing constellation? Six
types of involvement in the existing constellation
are specified by the horizonal structure: annihilating
totalization, relegating totalization, self-abandoning
capitulation, subservient capitulation, collaboration,
and resistance. What, then, is the nature of my involvement? Do I share with Plato, for example, the
view that only the philosopher is qualified to conduct
the affairs of the state? Do I hold the view that
the role of philosophy is to serve as a handmaiden
to natural science? Do I see myself as among the
last of the philosophers, as presiding over the final
stages of the subsumption of philosophy by natural
science? Such questions as these must be raised and
answered in the context provided by the answer to
the first question. If it is true that a collaborative
constellation exists, then my own stance must be
that of a collaborator. Similarly, if a reductionist
constellation exists, my stance must be that of a
totalizer or a capitulator. Finally, if a heterogeneous constellation exists, it is possible that
I am resisting, totalizing, or capitulating. While
the second question is raised and answered in the
context of the answer to the first, its answer is
not a mere deduction from the first answer. It may
appear to be so if the existing constellation is
collaborative, for example; but deductions are impersonal and indifferent to value, and the process of
self-orientation is not.

The two questions which promote reflective disengagement are raised in the context of an intention
to answer the ultimate question of self-orientation.
The two questions can be raised as though they were
sociological questions, for example. If the horizonal
structure were appropriated by sociologists, then
investigators of society may inquire whether the
existing constellation is reductionist, collaborative,
or heterogeneous. They could appeal to the charts
in Chapter III in order to determine just what horizonal configuration exists. However, when the question
is raised in this manner it is not an operation on
the level of responsibility; rather, it is an operation on the level of intelligence. Because the question is raised on the level of responsibility in
the present context, its emergence is attended by
an interest in self-orientation. Its significance
lies, not simply in its intention of an understanding
of the nature of the existing constellation, but
in its function as facilitating an eventual determination of my own stance. Similarly, the question of
my own stance may be asked for its own sake, and
how I happen to stand in the constellation becomes
simply a question of fact. But, if this question
is raised without the intention of self-orientation,
it is raised without a sense of the impact the answer
might have upon my own cultural involvement in the
future. Deliberative activity presupposes a reflective acknowledgement of the possibility that, as
a consequence of my deliberative reflections, I might
have to change. If this sense of the possible impact
of my questioning on my way of life is lacking, the
thoroughness of my self-questioning may be affected.
Psychologically, the sense of possible impact may
drive me away from self-study altogether; on the
other hand, barring psychological aberrations and
supposing a genuine interest in self-orientation,
the sense of possible impact may motivate me to inquire of myself with great thoroughness.

The two questions which promote reflective disengagement and block immediate accommodation of internal
perplexity are not the detached and disinterested
questions of natural or human science. They are exis-
tential questions raised in the context of an intention to orientate myself in my culture. The overarch-
ing context is provided by the ultimate question
of the deliberative process toward which I am heading:
How should I stand in the existing constellation?

2.2. EVALUATION: WEIGHING THE OPTIONS

The evaluative phase of the process of self-orientation may be divided into three inter-penetrating moments. The entire evaluative phase heads toward a judgment of the type: It is most worthwhile for me to participate in the existing constellation in this way. Accordingly, in the first moment of the evaluative phase I ask myself, What is the ideal of my horizon? In order to determine which type of activity specified by the horizonal structure is most worthwhile for me qua philosopher to pursue, I must first determine the nature of the philosophic horizon to my satisfaction. In the second moment of the evaluative phase I raise the rational question of consistency: Is the ideal of my horizon consistent with one of the two cultural ideals? Given the ideal of my horizon, does the pursuit of one of these ideals involve me in a performative self-contradiction? In the third moment of the evaluative phase I raise two affective questions of value: (i) Is the pursuit of philosophy as defined worthwhile? (ii) Is the type of cultural participation which I have found to be consistent with the ideal of philosophy worthwhile? Both of these questions are intended to bring to light my affective orientation and to promote reflection on my affective responses to the ideal of my horizon and to the two cultural ideals.

2.2.1. THE NATURE OF PHILOSOPHY

By the nature of philosophy is meant its ideal, mode of operation, and world. Of particular importance here is the philosophic ideal; for it is against the philosophic ideal that the consistency or inconsistency of the options is to be weighed. It is to be noted at this point that adequate reflection on the nature of the philosophic horizon requires a concerted effort to maintain the dissolution of previous involvement that was brought about by the recognition of horizonal dissonance. As self-orientating reflection in general occurs in the interval between spontaneous involvement and deliberate involvement, so deliberative reflection on the nature of my horizon, being a part of the process of self-orientation, takes place in that interval as well. Accordingly, the question at hand is not analogous to the second question of the earlier deliberative phase. It is not my previous spontaneous activity that I am seeking

to understand; rather, I am seeking to grasp the
nature of my horizon which may or may not have been
expressed coherently in my previous spontaneous involvement.

What is the nature of the philosophic horizon? The
data relevant to answering this question seem to
be of two types, internal and external. Internal
data are data obtained by adverting to relevant data
of consciousness, that is, myself as philosophic
-- my ideal, mode of operation, and world. External
data are data obtained by adverting to past and contemporary philosophic expression. To answer the question of philosophy's nature, I advert to the history
of philosophy and to my own operations in alternation.
By adverting to the history of philosophy I call
forth in myself the philosophic mode of operation
as data of consciousness; by adverting to data of
consciousness I augment the merely lived experience
of my philosophic mode with understanding and formulation. Again, by adverting to the historical opinions
of philosophers on the nature of philosophy, my own
opinions are called forth; then, by adverting to
myself, I subject those spontaneous opinions to reflective scrutiny.

This alternation of advertence from external
to internal data and back again depends for its efficacy upon the spontaneity of subjectivity itself.
Naturally, the danger of subjectivistic conclusions
arises. But two ranges of spontaneous tendencies
may be distinguished. On the one hand, there are
those tendencies which are properly named biases;
on the other hand, there are those upon which we
inevitably rely in every attempt to overcome our
biases. There is no escaping the fact that the pursuit of answers to questions is always a subjective
activity in the neutral sense of 'subjective'. The
problem, then, is not that this process is subjective,
but that one range of subjective tendencies may interfere with another range. Consequently, if we ask
what the criterion of judgment is that is relevant
to this process of discovering the nature of philosophy, we are asking about the tendencies constitutive
of the deep mode of operation. But the question regarding the nature of the deep mode must also be
raised in ignorance of the nature of the deep mode;
in pursuing the grounds of objectivity we must rely
upon the spontaneities of subjectivity. Accordingly,
the model of deliberation being constructed is de-

signed to provide the opportunity for one range of spontaneous tendencies to overwhelm the other; it is hoped that those tendencies which lead us to objective conclusions will prevail. Nevertheless, several tendencies which may interfere with the clarifying alternation of advertence may be considered.

First, I may believe that the question of philosophy's nature is perennial, and this belief may undermine the deliberative process. The everlasting character of the question may be interpreted in at least two ways. On the one hand, it may be taken to mean that the question of philosophy's nature cannot be answered, that its answer is absolutely beyond my grasp. On the other hand, it may be taken to mean that the answer is very difficult to obtain, but that I may expect to approximate to it gradually. Naturally, if I hold the first interpretation, there is no point to my continuing my inquiry. But, if I hold the second interpretation, there is reason to continue; after all, even the natural sciences claim only to approximate to the truth. However, both of these interpretations are somewhat abstract. Concretely, the question of philosophy's nature is raised by each philosopher; moreover, each philosopher has in fact answered the question for himself with greater or less circumspection. Just as philosophers adhere, either implicitly or explicitly, to some ideal of cultural unity, so they adhere more or less reflectively to some ideal of philosophic success. Philosophers may express with frequency their bewilderment, their confusion, their wonder, their awe; but, for the most part, they claim to have some idea of what they are doing. This 'idea' lies among the internal data to be considered reflectively.

Second, I may be too selective in my approach to external data. Relevant external data are multiform. The informative alternation of my advertence from internal to external data and back again may be inhibited by intruding internal commitments. By their nature, internal data do not wait passively for me to integrate them into my reflections; for they are my operations, my beliefs, my commitments. Just as I may subject myself to reflective scrutiny, so also may I skew my reflections, rendering them overly selective.[4] When I turn to investigate the external data relevant to the determination of philosophy's nature, I may fail to maintain reflective disengagement. For example, having been previously

122

a phenomenologist, I may refuse to admit logical empiricism into the philosophic fold. Employing the model, I may reason that logical empiricism has capitulated to totalizing natural science and, therefore, could not be an instance of philosophy. Again, having been previously a linguistic analyst, I may refuse to view seriously the products of Continental idealism. I may reason that idealism is resisting irrationally the subservient philosophic role. However, it is to be recalled that totalization, capitulation, collaboration, and resistance are not evidence of the agency of particular horizons; any of the six horizons presently existing may totalize, capitulate, collaborate, or resist. Moreover, a single horizon in a particular period may be internally differentiated -- partially resisting, partially capitulating, partially totalizing. To avoid excessive selectivity in my approach to external data, I must achieve the high altitude of surveillance characteristic of the historian of contemporary philosophy.[5]

Third, I may object that philosophy has no single nature. The implications of this extremely abstract position go beyond the discontinuation of the deliberative process and call into question the unity of the philosophic horizon itself. The position is extremely abstract. A remark of Hegel's, made in the introduction to his <u>History of Philosophy</u>, is to the point.

> However different the philosophies have been, they had a common bond in that they were philosophy. Thus whoever may have studied or become acquainted with a philosophy, of whatever kind, provided only that it is such, has thereby become acquainted with philosophy. That delusive mode of reasoning which regards diversity alone, and from doubt of or aversion to the particular form in which a universal finds its actuality, will not grasp or even allow this universal nature, I have elsewhere likened to an invalid recommended by the doctor to eat fruit, and who has cherries, plums, or grapes, before him, but who pedantically refuses to take anything because no part of what is offered him is fruit, some of it being cherries, and the rest being plums or grapes.[6]

The deliberative process being outlined presently presupposes the horizonal structure. Consequently, the fundamental unity of the philosophic horizon

123

is presupposed by the question of philosophy's nature, and by 'nature' is meant "standpoint, mode of operation, and world". I must assume a single nature, anticipating in apparent diversity a common core.[7]

Fourth, I may object that I have no access to data of consciousness, that the invitation to exploit self-presence is merely an invitation to explore the domain of "mere subjectivity". The alternation of advertence, I may conclude, is an oscillation between objective observation and merely subjective whim. This objection takes exception to the emphasis I have placed upon the model as an <u>adequately heuristic</u> device [See Chapter II, Section 2.1.]. To be sustained, the objection must exclude from serious consideration two facts which I have attempted to acknowledge fully. First, there exist at least six horizons, each of which seems to employ its own criteria of objectivity and reality. It seems reasonable, consequently, to await the outcome of a study of these approaches before deciding that the criteria of objectivity and reality proper to one horizon are applicable to the study of the horizons themselves. Second, <u>general</u> linguistic usage reflects the more or less thorough, common exploitation of a given access to data of consciousness or internal data. Even natural scientists and ordinary subjects, those whom one might expect to adhere naturally to an approach which excludes advertence to internal data, employ words and phrases designating standpoints and modes of operation (worlds in their self-present dimensions). There seem to be no reasonable grounds for ignoring this fact when we set out to construct a model for the study of horizons. The objection, then, defends a more determinate, less openly heuristic approach to the study of horizons; and so it also begs the questions of horizonal adequacy and legitimacy. Moreover, it deprives the self-orientating philosopher of a range of data to which subjects of all other horizons commonly appeal with greater or less frequency.

The task of answering the question of philosophy's nature may seem monumental; indeed, it is the difficulty of this task which grounds the merely relative adequacy of conclusions and brings into relief the critical significance of the alternation of advertence from external to internal data and back again. External data are multiform; internal data are intrusive and elusive. There seems to be no infallible method

124

of insuring the correctness of my conclusion. Nevertheless, by maintaining conscientiously the reflective
disengagement of the deliberative process, the proba-
bility of a mistaken conclusion is reduced. Moreover,
in the second moment of the evaluative phase the
question of consistency arises; and in the third
moment there arise two questions of value. Throughout
these subsequent moments the conclusion arrived at
in the first moment remains merely hypothetical;
depending on their outcomes, its adequacy may be
further reinforced, further qualified, or completely
denied.[8] However, one should expect no more than
a relatively adequate conclusion to the question
of philosophy's nature; the history of philosophy
and its contemporary situation are complex affairs,
and self-clarification is perhaps a life-long enterprise. Moreover, like other horizons, the philosophic
horizon unfolds temporally; philosophy itself is
in process of development or decline. Accordingly,
the first moment of the evaluative phase need not
be specified further; in the end, each one must make
his relatively adequate judgment on the ideal of
philosophic activity for himself.

2.2.2. THE QUESTION OF CONSISTENCY

In the second moment of the evaluative phase
the question of consistency is raised. The nature
of my horizon having been determined tentatively,
the question of consistency takes the following form:
Is a particular ideal of cultural unity, and so also
a particular type of cultural involvement, consistent
with the ideal of my horizon? Specifically I ask,
Is reductionist activity consistent with the aims
of my horizon? Is collaborative activity consistent
with the aims of my horizon?

Is reductionist activity consistent with the
aims of my horizon? If I subscribe reflectively to
the ideal of logical empiricism, for example, I may
ask, Is the reductionist ideal of cultural unity
consistent with the ideal of philosophy as logical
empiricism? Again, is totalizing participation consistent? Is capitulating participation consistent? Is annihilating totalization more or less consistent than
relegating totalization? Is self-abandoning capitulation more or less consistent than subservient capitulation? Clearly, the question of consistency includes
a consideration of the roles of co-existing horizons.

If I find that capitulating participation is consistent with my philosophic ideal, I find as well that totalizing participation by a co-existing horizon is acceptable to me. As immediate accommodation includes a spontaneous positioning of co-existing horizons relative to one's own, so deliberate accommodation includes a reflective positioning of them.

Again, if I subscribe to the ideal of hermeneutic-dialectic philosophy, I may ask, Is the reductionist ideal of cultural unity consistent with the ideal of philosophy as hermeneutical and critical? Is totalizing participation consistent? Is capitulating participation consistent? Is annihilating totalization more or less consistent than relegating totalization? Is self-abandoning capitulation more or less consistent than subservient capitulation? The roles of co-existing horizons must be considered. If I find that one of these types of participation is consistent, I find as well that its complement in my constellation is acceptable to me.

Is collaborative activity consistent with the aims of my horizon? If I subscribe reflectively to the ideal of hermeneutic-dialectic philosophy, for example, I may ask, Is the collaborative ideal of cultural unity consistent with the hermeneutical and critical ideal? Is collaborative participation consistent? Is resistant participation consistent? I must note that if I find collaborative participation to be consistent, I find as well that totalization and capitulation are intolerable and that these types should not inform my constellation. Again, if I find that resistant participation is consistent, I find as well that my constellation includes at least one totalizing horizon.

If I subscribe reflectively to the ideal of logical empiricism, I may ask, Is the ideal of differentiated unity consistent with the logical empiricist ideal? Is collaborative participation consistent? Is resistant participation consistent? If collaborative participation is found to be consistent, totalizing and capitulating horizons are not acceptable. If resistant participation is found to be consistent, my constellation includes at least one totalizing horizon.

The conclusion reached in the second moment of the evaluative phase takes the following form:

This cultural ideal and this particular type of cultural involvement are consistent with the pursuit of the ideal of my horizon.

2.2.3. THE QUESTION OF VALUE

The third moment of the evaluative phase brings into focus my affective relation to the ideal of my horizon as defined and to the type of cultural participation I have found to be consistent with that ideal. The second moment alone does not provide adequate grounds for a decision. Consistency is primarily a cognitive criterion. Consequently, the second moment involved an abstraction from the affective relation I have to the ideal of my horizon and the ideals of cultural unity. It entitles me to conclude only that a particular type of cultural participation does not lead me to contradict performatively my horizonal ideal as defined. But I am not a purely cognitive being, and deliberation is not a purely cognitive process. In Lonergan's terms, for example, cognition involves the first three levels of conscious intentionality, while deliberation, evaluation and decision pertain to the fourth level. I am related to ideals not only cognitively but also through my feelings, affectively. Accordingly, even though the first moment of the evaluative phase took place in reflective disengagement, my cognitive determination of the nature of philosophy released in me an affective response.[10] The second moment, then, served only to relate the nature of philosophy as cognitively-determined to the ideals of cultural unity. The question of value of the third moment turns my attention to my affective relation to the ideal of philosophy I have specified, and also to my affective relation to the ideal of cultural unity with which it is consistent. Two questions are raised in the third moment: (i) Is the pursuit of philosophy as defined worthwhile? (ii) Is the type of cultural participation I have found to be consistent with my horizonal ideal worthwhile? By 'worthwhile' here I mean 'valued', that is, regarded highly, prized, or esteemed. Clearly, ideals may be valued for a variety of reasons, both adequate and inadequate; and what one happens to value may or may not be truly good. This moment of the evaluative phase is designed to facilitate the process of value-clarification and value-correction, without attempting to specify for the deliberating subject just which ideals are truly good and which

127

are not.

Is the pursuit of philosophy as defined worthwhile? Do I value the ideal of logical empiricism, for example? Do I value the ideal of hermeneutical and critical philosophy? Let us suppose I answer one of these specific questions in the affirmative: I do value the ideal of philosophy I have determined. Immediately I become suspicious of the conclusion I drew in the first moment. To what degree was my definition of philosophy simply a function of my feelings? I am moved to re-enact the first moment of the evaluative phase [See Section 2.2.1. above] with an expanded awareness of my preferences. Was my conclusion merely wish-fulfillment? Let us suppose, on the other hand, that I answer one of the specific questions in the negative: I do not value the ideal of philosophy I have determined. Again I become suspicious of my conclusion in the first moment, and I am moved to re-enact the process of inquiry into philosophy's nature. Now, however, I may be more directly suspicious of my feelings. Do my feelings accurately reflect true values? If they do, have I gone out of my way to contravene my own preferences, mistakenly assuming that all feelings are "merely subjective"? Have I made the mistake of seeking a conclusion that opposes my preferences simply because it opposes them? In short, both an affirmative and a negative conclusion to the first question of value lead to a re-enactment of the first moment of the evaluative phase.

Is the type of participation which I have found to be consistent with my horizonal ideal worthwhile? Do I value the ideal of reductionist unity? Do I value the ideal of differentiated unity? Let us suppose that pursuit of the reductionist ideal is consistent with the ideal of philosophy I determined originally, and that I answer the second question of value affirmatively: I do value the ideal of reductionist unity. Again I become suspicious of my original conclusion to the first moment. To what extent did my preference for a monolithic cultural unity inform and bias my inquiry into the nature of philosophy? Suppose, on the other hand, that I answer the second question of value negatively: I do not value the ideal of reductionist unity; totalizing and capitulating participation elicit from me the kind of affective response that signals a disvalue. Accordingly, I return to the first moment with a twofold suspicion.

128

Does the structure of my feelings require renovation?[11] On the other hand, have I made the mistake of seeking to contravene proleptically my preference for a particular type of cultural unity? Both negative and affirmative answers to the second question of value lead me to re-enact the first moment of the evaluative phase.

The third moment terminates in a judgment of the type: It is most worthwhile for me to participate in my constellation in this manner. However, this judgment is made subsequent to the completion of the internal dialogue between myself-as-feeling and myself-as-cognitive that is initiated when the two questions of value are raised. Naturally, the internal dialogue may be carried on indefinitely. The internal evidence that is appealed to in the first moment of the evaluative phase is elusive, and its range is expanded enormously when my affective orientation is included. The external evidence relevant to the first moment is multiform and complicated in each instance. Eventually, though, a line is to be drawn, the evaluative phase is to be concluded, a judgment of value is to be made.

2.3. DECISION: DELIBERATE ENGAGEMENT

Reflective disengagement from my constellation is a short-lived luxury. It may be enjoyed intermittently over a life-time, but it cannot be maintained continuously. I am called upon to choose and to participate in my culture along the lines of my choice. Both my judgment of value and my subsequent decision involve risk, for they rest on a knowledge of my horizon and of myself which is only relatively adequate at best. But such risks are at least calculated risks, and they are preferable to merely spontaneous participation in my culture.

The last phase of the deliberative process of self-orientation is constituted by the decision to participate in my constellation in the manner found most worthwhile in light of the enlightening dialogue of the evaluative phase. The decisive phase differs from previous phases in that it does not have its proper end in itself. Decision is a leap. In the decisive phase I engage once again in cultural activity; I effect a transition from reflective disengagement to cultural participation. This transition

129

is not a return to my original stance, the spontaneous
participation which was called into question when
my constellation became actual. It is the institution
of a new type of cultural participation, deliberate
participation. My involvement in my culture has been
rendered methodical by the deliberative process.
I know the configuration of the constellation in
which I stand; I know where I stood spontaneously;
I have determined to my satisfaction the nature of
my horizon; I have identified the consistent type
of participation; I have evaluated both my horizonal
ideal and the ideals of cultural unity; I have sub-
jected my conclusions and my affective responses
to the ongoing criticism of internal dialogue; finally,
I am called upon to conclude that I know well enough
where I ought to stand.

3. A PERSONAL ILLUSTRATION

The model of the process of self-orientation
is not to be followed slavishly like a recipe. In
fact, the alternation of advertence from external
to internal data and back again and the internal
dialogue which are essential to the model, as promoting the objectivity of the deliberating subject,
preclude exact imitation. It may be useful nevertheless to have an illustration to which one might
appeal for further clarification of the main phases
of the model. Properly speaking, the model is a series
of related questions. By placing my own conclusions
and values within its frame, it may be exhibited
as a series of related answers to those questions.
Considered as a set of related answers, the deliberative model becomes a set of orientating guidelines.
Deliberate accommodation of internal horizontal perplexity is the development by the deliberating subject
of a set of guidelines for his cultural participation.
What follows, then, is one philosopher's tentative
set of guidelines.

My purpose in presenting a personal illustration
is not argumentative. My interest lies in facilitating
a grasp of the structure of the model by exhibiting
it in another way. Accordingly, I shall not assemble
an abundance of internal and external evidence for
my position on the nature of philosophy. Nor shall
I trace the erratic course of my alternating advertence or record the raised and lowered voices of
the critically important dialogue of thought and
feeling.

Reflective Disengagement. What type of constellation exists? A heterogeneous constellation exists.
How do I stand in the constellation? I stand as resisting totalization and capitulation.

Evaluation: First Moment. What is the nature
of my horizon? The philosophic ideal is twofold.
In the first place, philosophy heads toward an intellectual integration of human endeavors. In the second
place, philosophy heads toward a concrete synthesis
of endeavoring subjects. The philosophic world is
also twofold. The world of philosophy as intellectual
integration is the full range of existing horizons.
The world of philosophy as concrete synthesis is
the full range of endeavoring subjects. The philosophic mode of operation is twofold. The mode of
philosophy as intellectual integration is identification, differentiation and correlation of existing
horizons. The mode of philosophy as concrete synthesis is the implementation of an intellectual integration in harmonizing social conduct. Both modes
of philosophy involve a methodical exploitation of
a given access to data of consciousness.

Evaluation: Second Moment. Pursuit of the reductionist ideal of cultural unity is not consistent
with the pursuit of the philosophic ideal of intellectual integration. An intellectual integration pre-
serves the integrity of the elements to be integrated.
Pursuit of the reductionist ideal is not consistent
with the pursuit of the philosophic ideal of concrete
synthesis. Concrete synthesis is a differentiated
unity, not a monolithic unity; horizonal differences
are preserved in a concrete synthesis. Pursuit of
the collaborative ideal is consistent with the pursuit
of philosophy as intellectual integration and as
concrete synthesis.

Evaluation: Third Moment. As a philosopher in
this heterogeneous constellation I should resist
totalization and capitulation in two ways. First,
I should pursue an intellectual integration of the
full range of existing horizons. Second, I should
pursue a concrete synthesis of the full range of
endeavoring subjects by implementing the intellectual
integration in harmonizing social conduct. The pursuit
of intellectual integration alone is an incomplete
realization of the philosophic ideal. The pursuit
of concrete synthesis without having attained previously an intellectual integration is presumptuous

131

conduct. The two phases of philosophy are reciprocally constitutive. In the ideal case, an intellectual integration is achieved and then implemented in harmonizing social conduct. Concretely, the ideals of philosophy are not realized sequentially but concomitantly. The second phase depends for its efficacy upon the first; but the first phase depends for its evidence and verification upon the second.

4. PRAXIS AT THE LEVEL OF THE TIMES

The process of self-orientation is, in one of its aspects, the reflective development of horizonal guidelines. But, more importantly, the process culminates in deliberate engagement in the cultural matrix which essentially transforms the matrix. If the process I have described has been undergone successfully, the self-orientating subject has considered thoroughly his present cultural situation and his place in it. His engagement constitutes praxis at the level of his times. The course of action which issues willfully from his decision is a response to what Max Scheler has named the demands of the present. His chosen course of action, then, warrants careful and precise formulation. In the present section I shall explore briefly my notion of second-phase philosophy as harmonizing social conduct based upon an intellectual integration of the standpoints, modes, and worlds of the full range of existing horizons.

4.1. HORIZONAL DIPLOMACY

First-phase philosophic activity is already familiar to students of philosophy. From the time of philosophy's emergence, philosophers have characterized themselves repeatedly as seekers after a synoptic view. However, the practical philosophic activity I have specified is not so familiar. For second-phase philosophic activity I propose the name "horizonal diplomacy". This name is not only less awkward than "second-phase philosophic activity", but it also calls to mind international diplomacy and evokes in that way an analogous understanding.

Diplomacy, in an ordinary sense, is the management of international relations by negotiation. Similarly, horizonal diplomacy is the management of horizonal

132

relations by tactful intervention in constellations. A-
gain, in a more technical sense, international diplomacy is the intelligent and tactful implementation
of a foreign policy in the conduct of official relations between the governments of independent states.[12]
Similarly, horizonal diplomacy is the methodical
implementation of an intellectual integration for
the promotion of collaborative relations between
subjects of autonomous horizons. Just as the international diplomatist practices on the basis afforded
by a study of the history of international negotiations, an analysis of treaties, and an investigation
of the ambitions, resources, and weaknesses of individual nations; so the horizonal diplomatist practices
on the basis afforded by a study of the history of
horizonal relations, an analysis of coalitions and
disputes, and an investigation of the ideals, modes
of operation, and worlds of existing horizons. Again,
international diplomacy, if it is collaborative,
is practiced with an appreciation of common interests.
The Greeks of the fifth century B.C. recognized an
implicit 'law' which was thought to be above immediate
national interests and momentary expediency; the
Romans employed a vague notion of ius naturale or
natural right. Similarly, horizonal diplomacy, because
it is collaborative, is practiced with an appreciation
of common interests; it is guided by a heuristic
notion of the basic horizon of human existence which
includes in its scope all perduring horizons. Besides
horizon specific ideals, there are the ideals of
human subjectivity in general; besides horizon-specific
modes, there is the deep mode; besides horizon-specific
worlds, there is the universe of being to which all
emergent horizons have a tendency to lay claim.

Besides the similarities there are differences.
For the most part, international diplomacy is practiced with specific national interests in mind. So
it is that even the earliest diplomatists, the heralds
of the Homeric period, were placed under the tutelage
of Hermes, symbol of charm, trickery and cunning.
In contrast, the horizonal diplomatist is not an
agent of a particular horizon. This is the paradox,
as it were, of philosophic activity. While the horizonal diplomatist is a philosopher, it is also true
that philosophy happens to be that horizon which
promotes a general, collaborative accommodation of
horizonal perplexity. The horizonal diplomatist stands
to co-existing horizons as a diplomatic agent of
the human world stands to co-existing nations. He

differs greatly, then, from Plato's philosopher who holds that our troubles will not cease unless philosophers become kings in our states.[13]

The analogy with international diplomacy conveys a general idea of the role I have in mind for the practical philosopher who has been relatively successful in his pursuit of an intellectual integration of human endeavors. I turn now to a consideration of the thing-itself which I envisage.

The occasion for the initiation of diplomatic activity is constituted by the emergence of horizonal perplexity in members of a constellation. For the horizonal diplomatist to promote collaborative relations successfully, he must block immediate accommodation of horizonal perplexity and promote deliberate accommodation. It may appear, then, that there is no need for the horizonal diplomatist in a collaborative constellation, on the one hand, and that there is no point of insertion for the horizonal diplomatist in a reductionist constellation, on the other. It seems that occasions for the initiation of diplomatic activity arise only in heterogeneous constellations, those constellations which include at least one totalizing horizon and at least one resisting horizon. However, this apparent limitation on the role of the horizonal diplomatist has its root in a static conception of constellations. Horizons are gradual developments of subjects; every culture, if it is to survive, must take appropriate measures to reproduce itself. Consequently, horizonal perplexity regularly emerges during the acculturation process in all types of constellations as developing subjects are introduced to existing extraordinary endeavors. In every constellation, there is a point of entry for the horizonal diplomatist in the educational process. Through this opening, there passes the <u>horizonal diplomatist-as-teacher</u>. In situations calling for diplomacy-as-teaching, the dispute to be mediated normally involves the ordinary horizon as one of its parties. Besides the diplomatist-as-teacher, there is the <u>diplomatist-as-instigator</u>. The philosopher in a predominantly reductionist constellation, who somehow discovers a basis for promoting collaborative relations, becomes himself a resisting subject. But, because he is a horizonal diplomatist, his resistance is a self-conscious instigation of horizonal perplexity in contemporaneous subjects; he exploits the paradox of philosophic activity to promote per-

plexity, block immediate accommodation, and promote
deliberate accommodation. Finally, reflection on
the nature of heterogeneous constellations gives
rise to the notion of the horizonal diplomatist-as-
mediator. In heterogeneous constellations the stage
is set regularly for diplomatic intervention; the
co-existence of totalizers, capitulators, and resisters
virtually guarantees the frequent emergence of perplexity not only in the educational process but also
in the recurrent interactions of the educated.

The horizonal diplomatist may function as a
teacher, as an instigator, and as a mediator in all
three types of constellations. But my own set of
guidelines includes the orientating judgment that
the existing constellation is heterogeneous. Consequently, the notion of horizonal diplomacy, which
has emerged from the same process of self-orientation,
is qualified by an emphasis upon mediation. What
are the steps to be taken by the horizonal diplomatist-
as-mediator? I envisage two stages of diplomacy-as-
mediation. The first stage is impersonal, empathic,
and definitive of the particular situation. The second
is interpersonal, communicative, and transformative
of the situation.

In the first stage the diplomatist identifies
the horizons of the perplexed subjects, distinguishes
them from one another, and relates them to one another.
This procedure is impersonal, for as yet the diplomatist has not entered into dialogue or discussion,
verbally or in writing. But the procedure is nevertheless empathic. The identification, distinction, and
relation of the horizons constitutive of the actual
constellation is at once a re-enactment of the dialogue or discussion which is heard or read and a
correlation of the meanings expressed by the participating subjects with the standpoints, modes, and
worlds distinguished and related previously in a
relatively adequate intellectual integration. Finally,
this procedure is definitive of the particular situation; for its conclusion is a judgment of the following type: The present situation is constituted by
horizons of this type which differ from one another
in these ways and are related to one another in these
other ways.

In the second stage of horizonal diplomacy-as-
mediation the diplomatist intervenes in the constellation; he enucleates the dispute by bringing to

light the deep mode informing the horizon-specific modes, the ideals of subjectivity reflected in the horizon-specific ideals, and the universe of being partially objectified in the horizon-specific worlds; he transposes horizon-relative expressions from one horizon to another by adverting to the horizon-relative employments of key variable terms such as 'being', 'object', 'objectivity', 'knowing', and 'knowledge'. This procedure is interpersonal and communicative, for it is an engagement in the dialogue or discussion through the expression of meanings, verbally or in writing. It is transformative of the particular situation, first, because it is a complexification of the constellation by the addition of an explicitly collaborative member and, second, because enucleation and transposition, if successful, have mediated a common, rudimentary realization that collaboration could displace conflict in the future.

Clearly, the task of the horizonal diplomatist is not an easy one. It is more complicated than the complex task of conceptual analysis and linguistic clarification which has won the hearts and engrossed the minds of so many philosophers in our century. The conflicts with which the diplomatist is concerned have deeper roots than conceptual confusion and imprecise use of language. As I noted early in the present essay, some of the imprecise usages of ordinary subjects are rooted in the very nature of the ordinary horizon [See Chapter I, Section 8.4.]. The advocacy by philosophers of their total elimination is a consequence of an oversight of the significance of the horizonal variable. Again, the task of the horizonal diplomatist is more difficult than the task of communicating a body of 'truths'. There is a sense in which an intellectual integration may be called a body of truths, but the diplomatist's task is not its communication but its implementation in an indefinite range of particular situations. Perhaps the greatest difficulty associated with the practice of horizonal diplomacy derives from its dramatic nature. Diplomacy is a kind of performance which makes far-reaching demands upon the performer. The stance of the horizonal diplomatist is a precarious posture, one requiring simultaneous detachment and involvement. When the diplomatist intervenes, he complexifies the constellation, he becomes part of it, and the paradox of philosophic activity is easily transformed into an oscillation between deliberately collaborative implementation of an integration and virtually totalizing activity designed to impress the participants of philosophy's relevance to cultural life. Consequently, just as the international diplomatist, ideally, should be calm, accurate, patient, good-tempered, and modest, so too should the horizonal diplomatist be psychologically well-adjusted.[14] For the horizonal diplomatist is, above all, an exemplar of possible success in the transformation of contentious heterogeneity into collaborative unity in human endeavor. The relationship between psychological constitution and practical philosophic efficacy, it seems to me, cannot be ignored by aspiring practitioners of horizonal diplomacy. As Otto Bird has noted in his study, Cultures in Conflict, the imperialism typical of adherents of intellectual ideals has had its root invariably in hubris.[15]

Horizonal diplomacy may not be an easy task, but it is nevertheless demanded by the contemporary cultural situation. Returning to our analogy, modern international diplomacy, as the art of negotiation, first acquired a significant place in the political sphere during the thirteenth and fourteenth centuries in Italy because the conditions were favorable. It was inevitable, Sir Harold Nicolson has argued, that Italy should have become the mother of professional diplomacy. The Italian city states "were interconnected by countless common interests as well as sundered by ferocious rivalries; they were constantly engaged in a competition for power and preoccupied by those combinations and alliances which might render that power predominant."[16] Similarly, while the horizonal constellation has been complex for centuries, only recently has the complexity become explicitly sixfold. Moreover, our constellation, I have suggested, is heterogeneous; proponents of interdisciplinary studies are barely heard above the clamor of totalizers and resisters. As this heterogeneity becomes more acute, the need for horizonal diplomacy or some basically similar philosophic praxis becomes more urgent. Whole bodies of expression, whole meaningful worlds, whole modes of inquiry, discovery and creativity, and whole sets of ideals stand in danger of being discarded. Only the subject of that horizon whose world is the full range of horizons is specifically suited to methodically and equitably restore the balance.

Philosophy as intellectual integration of the arts and sciences has long been recognized as a separate pursuit. Philosophy as pursuit of the unity of science has also acquired a distinct place. But philosophy as concrete synthesis has yet to receive full recognition as a distinct philosophic activity deserving serious reflection and clear delineation. As international diplomacy was associated for many centuries with the preservation of archives, the analysis of treaties, and the study of the history of negotiations, so properly philosophic activity has been associated, virtually to this day, with the study of horizons and their relations. It was not until 1815 at the Congress of Vienna, long after the heralds and persuasive orators had been displaced by diplomatists, that the rules, conventions and presumptions of international diplomacy as the actual conduct of international relations were given a definite if fragile form. Second-phase philosophy has yet to reach a similar level of self-consciousness. In light of the disheartening collapses of intellectual monuments, this deficiency is somewhat understandable. One can hardly proceed confidently to enunciate in detail the canons of horizonal diplomacy if guiding intellectual integrations remain controversial. However, inattention to second-phase philosophy is rooted partially in an expectation of the ideal case of sequentially-ordered phases. In fact, the phases are reciprocally constitutive, just as negotiation and foreign policy are mutually transformative. Horizonal diplomacy is the implementation of an intellectual integration; but it is concretely the manner in which evidence is obtained and tentative integrations are tested. This concrete apprehension of the reciprocity of phases, however, is only a partial solution to the problem of elaborating and legitimating second-phase philosophy. What is needed is a heuristic device which permits us to draw conclusions about second-phase philosophy despite the absence of a generally-accepted intellectual integration. The horizonal structure developed in this essay is one such device.

As a testament to the need for an elaboration and legitimation of second-phase philosophy we have the perduring symbol of Socrates. Even though Socrates' death illustrates the need for serious reflection upon the canons of practical philosophy, other elements of the Socratic symbol tend to obscure that need. Nowadays the symbol of Socrates is recalled to console us. A most distressing question recurs within philosophy and outside it: What is philosophy? In our internal dialogues the Socratic symbol is recalled to support us in a poorly-defined pursuit, to inspire us, and to renew us. In fact, the death of Socrates, rather than stimulating reflection on the canons of practical philosophy as it should, seems to function as an indirect confirmation of a conviction of our profundity and the inability of the ordinary mortal to understand us.[17] In our conversations with non-philosophers, on the other hand, the Socratic symbol is employed to help others situate us. To the Socratic symbol as a consoling, inspiring, and renewing force in our philosophic lives I have no serious objections; but the use of the symbol as a situating device has its drawbacks. First of all, the symbol as such is ambiguous. Socrates is synoptic inquiry; but he is also perduring aporia. He exemplifies the ideal of philosophy's first phase; but he also exemplifies the pursuit of that ideal as virtually interminable. Second, Socrates symbolizes emergent philosophy; but modern philosophy is a variety of activities rooted in centuries of wondering. Third, Socrates practiced in a constellation with a relatively low level of complexity; but the present constellation, it seems, has a sixfold complexity. Fourth, Plato's Socrates of the Republic reflected at length on the problems attendant upon the implementation of a reductionist integration; but the perdurance and resilience of a multiplicity of horizons constitutes a serious challenge to the adequacy of the reductionist ideal of cultural unity. As a situating device, the Socratic symbol may have outlived its usefulness. While the memory of Socrates may orient, inspire, and renew the philosophic enterprise, it may inhibit it as well by providing a symbolic justification, as it were, of our inattentiveness to second-phase philosophic activity. The philosophic horizon awaits its own version of the diplomatists' Congress of Vienna. But it seems certain that such a congress will lack direction and cohesion unless the horizonal structure or a similar model is commonly employed to provide boundaries for common reflection.[18]

The task of the horizonal diplomatist is difficult and demanded by our times, but horizonal diplomacy is not a panacea. The activities of identification, distinction, relation, intervention, enucleation, and transposition are undertaken in the atmosphere of a selective attention to the horizonal variable. But the horizonal variable is just one among many which must be taken into account in the pursuit of a complete understanding and adequate resolution of the conflicts that fragment the cultural community. As the horizonal diplomatist must abide in the paradox of philosophic activity, so he must retain and nourish an awareness of just what he can and cannot accomplish.

The ideal governing horizonal diplomacy is cosmopolitan rather than utopian. H. G. Wells interpreted the drama of world history as the tension between man's animal affection for the narrow comforts of tribe and village and his self-surpassing or over-reaching search for the widest possible community of thought, wealth, and work. W. Warren Wagar has translated this distinction into the antithesis between Utopia and Cosmopolis.[19] If the ideal governing horizonal diplomacy were utopian in this sense, then horizonal diplomacy would be more appropriately named philosophic totalization. The process of creating a utopia, like the process of totalizing a horizon, is a terminal process; the aim of the process is a relatively static, monolithic unity. As monolithic cultural unity is characterized by the totalization of the ideals, mode, and world of a single horizon, so utopian unity is characterized by parochialism and ethnocentrism.[20] On the other hand, the process of creating a cosmopolis, like the process of promoting differentiated cultural unity, is open-ended and never-ending. Wagar writes that cosmopolis

is the quintessence of a civilization, the gathering of all its vital human resources into a living organic unity. A cosmopolis is not a utopia; it is not the best of all possible worlds, but the boundless community of the best in the world-that-is . . .. Cosmopolis is simply the world in a state of optimal integration.[21]

It follows that, as horizonal diplomacy differs from horizonal totalization, it differs also from that terminal process by which the personal and interpersonal tensions generated by self-surpassing encounters are supposed to be eliminated.

Again, my description of philosophy as a two-stage process is ideal-typical, and so it differs from what is meant by the popular notion of a utopian scheme. Numerous problems attend the pursuit of an intellectual integration, and these problems are intellectual, psychological, and social. Moreover, any intellectual integration will be historically

relative in some of its aspects, that is, it will
be partially a response to the issues that happen
to arise in a particular historical period. Again,
horizonal diplomacy has been conceived in abstraction
from personality and class differences, differences
of the level of mastery of an existing intellectual
integration, and differences of the level of facility
with which an existing integration is tested and
verified as it is transposed to actual practice.
As the horizonal structure itself is only a heuristic
device to be employed in the study of internal cultural relations and for horizonal self-orientation,
so the conception of horizonal diplomacy is only
an ideal-type useful for exposing the virtual tendencies of the philosophic horizon. Actual discrep-
ancies can be identified and investigated in the
light of this ideal-type. Utopian schemes, on the
other hand, tend to force signs of failure into the
shadows.[22]

Finally, Karl Mannheim introduced, early in
the present century, a notion of utopia which differs
from Wagar's technical notion and from the popular
notion of a utopian scheme.

A state of mind is utopian when it is incongruous
with the state of reality within which it occurs.[23]

By analogy, a conception is utopian when its implementation implies a reconstitution of the existing order.
The notion of horizonal diplomacy is a conception
of a manner in which both philosophy and the horizonal situation generally might be renovated. As
such it is a utopian conception in Mannheim's sense.

In this chapter, and in those preceding, I have
attempted to accomplish a preparatory maneuver. I
have not assaulted the citadel which hides the required intellectual integration from our view. My
limited aim has been to present a model which may
be useful to students of culture and, especially,
to the disorientated philosopher. It is important
that the limitations of my attempt be fully appreci-
ated. To that end, and as a final note, I shall direct
attention once more to the nature and uses of a model
as described by Bernard Lonergan.

For models purport to be, not descriptions of
reality, not hypotheses about reality, but simply

141

interlocking sets of terms and relations. Such sets, in fact, turn out to be useful in guiding investigations, in framing hypotheses, and in writing descriptions. Thus, a model will direct the attention of an investigator in a determinate direction with either of two results: it may provide him with a basic sketch of what he finds to be the case; or it may prove largely irrelevant, yet the discovery of this irrelevance may be the occasion of uncovering clues that otherwise might be overlooked. Again, when one possesses models, the task of framing an hypothesis is reduced to the simpler matter of tailoring a model to suit a given object or area. Finally, the utility of the model may arise when it comes to describing a known reality. For known realities can be exceedingly complicated, and an adequate language to describe them hard to come by. So the formulation of models and their general acceptance as models can facilitate enormously both description and communication.[24]

NOTES TO CHAPTER IV

[1]Lonergan, Method in Theology, p. 9.

[2]Ibid., pp. 13-14.

[3]See Insight, xiii, xxx, pp. 390-396, 421.

[4]For a brief account of the process of selective inattention, see Patrick Mullahy, Oedipus: Myth and Complex (New York: Grove Press, 1948), pp. 299-300. For a more detailed discussion, see Harry Stack Sullivan, The Interpersonal Theory of Psychiatry, eds. Helen Swick Perry and Mary Ladd Gawel (New York: W. W. Norton, 1953), pp. 161-164, 232-234.

[5]This altitude is achieved with varying degrees of success by a variety of historians of contemporary philosophy. Each of the following historians distinguishes at least two major trends in contemporary philosophic thought. While they may differ from one another in their evaluations of the philosophic adequacy of the trends, they all share an awareness of contemporary philosophic diversity. See Gerard Radnitzky, Contemporary Schools of Metascience (Chicago: Henry Regnery, 1970), pp. 15-17; Wolf-

gang Stegmuller, <u>Main Currents in Contemporary German, British,</u> <u>and American Philosophy</u> (Bloomington: Indiana University Press, 1970), pp. 13-14; John Passmore, <u>A Hundred Years of Philosophy</u> (Harmondsworth: Penguin Books, 1968), pp. 466-467, 477-479; I. M. Bochenski, <u>Contemporary European Philosophy</u>, trans. Donald Nicholl and Karl Aschenbrenner (Berkeley: University of California Press, 1965), pp. 30-38; F. C. Copleston, <u>Contemporary Philosophy</u>: <u>Studies of Logical Positivism and Existentialism</u> (Westminster: The Newman Press, 1956), pp. 22, 125, 129-130; E. A. Burtt, <u>In Search of Philosophic Understanding</u> (New York: The New American Library, 1965), Chaps. 2-5; K.-O. Apel, <u>Towards a Transforma-</u> <u>tion of Philosophy</u>, trans. Glyn Adey and David Frisby (London: Routledge & Kegan Paul, 1980), Chap. 2; Richard Rorty, <u>Philosophy and the Mirror of Nature</u> (Princeton: Princeton University Press, 1979), Part Three; Richard Rorty, <u>Consequences</u> <u>of Pragmatism (Essays: 1972-1980)</u> (Minneapolis: University of Minnesota Press, 1982), Introduction.

⁶G. W. F. Hegel, <u>On Art, Religion, Philosophy: Introductory</u> <u>Lectures to the Realm of Absolute Spirit</u>, ed. J. Glenn Gray (New York: Harper Torchbooks, 1970), p. 226.

⁷Naturally, this assumption may be disputed by many philosophers. A single standpoint, mode, and world does not in fact characterize contemporary, modern, or ancient philosophy. Two points are to be noted. First of all, advertence to internal data includes in its sweep one's own ideals <u>qua</u> philosopher. It follows that the process of determining philosophy's nature involves not only an appeal to philosophy as practiced but to philosophy as one <u>would like</u> it to be practiced. Consequently, the obvious diversity in modes of operation may be offset by the discovery of a unity of aspiration. Second, philosophy as currently practiced may be totalizing, capitulating, collaborating, or resisting; and each of these types of cultural participation qualifies or alters to varying degrees the philosophic mode of operation. It follows that the empirical grounds to which one appeals to deny a single philosophic nature may only be evidence of philosophy's present plight. For a survey of contemporary philosophers' views of themselves and our present philosophic needs, see <u>The Owl of Minerva: Philosophers on Philo-</u> <u>sophy</u>, eds. Charles J. Bontempo and S. Jack Odell (New York: McGraw-Hill, 1975). See also the conceptions of the philosopher presented by Peter Winch in <u>The Idea of a Social Science and</u> <u>Its Relation to Philosophy</u> (London: Routledge & Kegan Paul, 1958), pp. 4-10. For a sociologist's view of currently fashionable philosophy, with particular regard to its relation to the ideal of intellectual integration or metaphysics, see Ernest Gellner, "The Crisis in the Humanities and the Mainstream of Philosophy," in <u>Crisis in the Humanities</u>, ed. J. H. Plumb (Harmondsworth: Penguin Books, 1964), pp. 45-81. In support of my

suggestion that philosophic performance may not be pure and unmixed, see Gellner's conclusion that contemporary philosophy in the Anglo-Saxon tradition "provides or services the basic conceptual equipment of humanist thought" (pp. 70-71).

[8] It is important to note that the deliberative model being developed is intended not only to accommodate but also to promote the self-correcting process of devising horizonal guidelines. The explicit acknowledgement of the positive contribution to self-orientation made by reflective retrogression or reversion to less complex stages of the deliberative process constitutes a fundamental feature of this model.

[9] For clarificatory purposes, in this section I shall employ Radnitzky's division of contemporary philosophy into Anglo-Saxon philosophy as ordinary language philosophy and logical empiricism, on the one hand, and Continental philosophy as hermeneutic-dialectic philosophy on the other.

[10] On feelings as intentional responses to values, see Lonergan, Method in Theology, pp. 30-34.

[11] See Max Scheler, Ressentiment, trans. William W. Holdheim (New York: Schocken Books, 1972), on perversion of values. See also Abraham Maslow, The Farther Reaches of Human Nature (New York: The Viking Press, 1972), pp. 36-37 on 'counter-valuing'.

[12] The definition is that of Sir Ernest Satow. It is quoted by Sir Harold Nicolson, Diplomacy (London: Oxford University Press, 1969), pp. 24, 122. In the present section I shall rely upon Nicolson's account of the development of organized international diplomacy. See pp. 1-14 of his essay.

[13] Republic 473c-e.

[14] Nicolson, Diplomacy, pp. 62-63. As the psychological therapist should be psychologically healthy, so the horizonal diplomatist should be well-adjusted. However, horizonal diplomacy is not to be conceived strictly as a type of therapy, except insofar as it is governed by the following guideline: "The therapist's skill and art lie in keeping things simple enough so that something can happen: in other words, he clears the field for favorable change, and then tries to avoid getting in the way of its development." See H. S. Sullivan, The Psychiatric Interview, eds. Helen Swick Perry and Mary Ladd Gawel (New York: W. W. Norton, 1970), p. 227. Psychological constitution has its effects in cognitive work also; consequently, the philosopher's psychological constitution may have a detrimental influence upon his pursuit of an intellectual integration. See Maslow's list of cognitive pathologies in The Psychology of

Science: A Reconnaissance (Chicago: Henry Regnery Company, 1969), pp. 26-29.

[15] Otto Bird, Cultures in Conflict, pp. 178-184. See also E. A. Burtt's general call for philosophic attention to the psychological in In Search of Philosophic Understanding, pp.310-311: "The form of awareness that urgently needs to expand is awareness of the deep-seated motivations active in one's relation to other people, for they are the forces decisively affecting man for weal or for woe."

[16]Nicolson, Diplomacy, pp. 12-13.

[17] As Hannah Arendt has noted, "The reason Plato wanted the philosopher to become the ruler of the city lay in the conflict between the philosopher and the polis, or in the hostility of the polis toward philosophy, which probably had lain dormant for some time before it showed its immediate threat to the life of the philosopher in the trial and death of Socrates. Politically, Plato's philosophy shows the rebellion of the philosopher against the polis. The philosopher announces his claim to rule, but not so much for the sake of the polis and politics (although patriotic motivation cannot be denied in Plato and distinguishes his philosophy from those of his followers in antiquity) as for the sake of philosophy and the safety of the philosopher." See Between Past and Future, p. 107.

[18] I do not mean to imply that the Socratic method should be excluded from consideration when we pursue an adequate notion of second-phase philosophic activity. However, it remains that we must be attentive to the possible disadvantages of motivating and governing our actual performance by adverting to the symbol of Socrates. As Lonergan has noted, feelings are evoked by symbols, and they provide the mass, momentum, and drive of our conscious and intentional activity. See Method in Theology, p. 65; see also Insight, pp. 188-189, 195, 237.

[19] W. Warren Wagar, The City of Man. Prophecies of a World Civilization in Twentieth-Century Thought (Baltimore: Penguin Books, 1967), p. 14.

[20]Ibid., pp. 13-17.

[21]Ibid., p. 15.

[22] For a general discussion of typologies and their uses, see Edward A.Tiryakian, "Typologies," in International Encyclopaedia of the Social Sciences, pp. 177-185.

[23]Karl Mannheim, Ideology and Utopia, pp. 192-193.

[24]Lonergan, Method in Theology, pp. 284-285.

BIBLIOGRAPHY

Adler, Mortimer. How To Read a Book. New York: Simon and Schuster, 1940.

Apel, K.-O. Towards a Transformation of Philosophy. London: Routledge & Kegan Paul, 1980.

Arendt, Hannah. Between Past and Future: Eight Exercises in Political Thought. New York: The Viking Press, 1961.

-----. The Human Condition. Garden City: Doubleday, 1959.

Aristotle. De Anima.

-----. Metaphysics.

-----. Nicomachean Ethics.

-----. Politics.

Artz, Johannes. "Newman as Philosopher". International Philosophical Quarterly 16 (1976).

Barth, Hans. Truth and Ideology. Trans. Frederic Lilge. Berkeley: University of California Press, 1976.

Barzun, Jacques. The House of Intellect. New York: Harper, 1959.

Bellah, Robert N. "To Kill and Survive or To Die and Become: The Active Life and the Contemplative Life as Ways of Being Adult". Daedalus (Spring 1976).

Benda, Julien. The Betrayal of the Intellectuals. Trans. Richard Aldington. Boston: Beacon Press, 1955.

Bernstein, Richard J. Praxis and Action: Contemporary Philosophies of Human Activity. Philadelphia: University of Pennsylvania Press, 1971.

Biddis, Michael D. The Age of the Masses. Harmondsworth: Penguin, 1977.

Bird, Otto. Cultures in Conflict: An Essay in the Philosophy of the Humanities. Notre Dame, London: University of Notre Dame Press, 1976.

Bochenski, I. M. Contemporary European Philosophy. Trans. Donald Nicholl and Karl Aschenbrenner. Berkeley: University of

California Press, 1965.

Bontempo, Charles, and S. Jack Odell, eds. The Owl of Minerva: Philosophers on Philosophy. New York: McGraw-Hill, 1975.

Burtt, E. A. In Search of Philosophic Understanding. New York: The New American Library, 1965.

-----. The Metaphysical Foundations of Modern Science. Garden City: Doubleday, 1954.

Carlyle, Thomas. Thomas Carlyle: Selected Writings. Ed. Alan Shelston. Harmondsworth: Penguin, 1971.

Cassirer, Ernst. The Philosophy of Symbolic Forms, Vol. III. Trans. Ralph Mannheim. London: Yale University Press, 1957.

Chesterton, G. K. The Common Man. London: Sheed and Ward, 1950.

Collingwood, R. G. Speculum Mentis, or the Map of Knowledge. Oxford: Clarendon Press, 1924, 1970.

Commoner, Barry. The Closing Circle. New York: Alfred A. Knopf, 1971.

Copleston, F. C. Contemporary Philosophy: Studies of Logical Positivism and Existentialism. Westminster: The Newman Press, 1956.

Darwin, Charles. The Expression of the Emotions in Man and Animals. Chicago, London: The University of Chicago Press, 1965.

Dawson, Christopher. The Age of the Gods. London, New York: Sheed and Ward, 1933.

Dilthey, Wilhelm. Pattern and Meaning in History. Ed. H. P. Rickman. New York: Harper and Row, 1962.

Eddington, Sir Arthur. New Pathways in Science. Cambridge: Camridge University Press, 1947.

-----. The Nature of the Physical World. Cambridge: Cambridge University Press, 1928.

Eliot, T. S. Christianity and Culture. New York: Harcourt, Brace & World, 1940.

Fichte, J. G. Fichte: Science of Knowledge (Wissenschaftslehre). Eds. and trans. Peter Heath and John Lachs. New York: Appleton-Century-Croft, 1970.

147

Freedman, Robert, ed. Marxist Social Thought. New York: Harcourt, Brace & World, 1968.

Freud, Sigmund. New Introductory Lectures on Psychoanalysis. Trans. James Strachey. Harmondsworth: Penguin, 1973.

-----. The Future of an Illusion. Trans. W. D. Robson-Scott. New York: Anchor Books, 1964.

Gellner, Ernest. "The Crisis in the Humanities and the Mainstream of Philosophy". In Crisis in the Humanities, ed. J. H. Plumb. Harmondsworth: Penguin, 1964.

Guerriere, Daniel. "The Structure of Mythic Existence". The Personalist (Summer 1974).

Gadamer, H.-G. Philosophical Hermeneutics. Trans. and ed. David E. Linge. Berkeley: University of California Press, 1976.

Hanson, F. Allan. "Meaning in Culture". In The Concept and Dynamics of Culture. Ed. Bernardo Bernardi. The Hague; Paris: Moulton Publishers, 1977.

Hegel, G. W. F. On Art, Religion, Philosophy: Introductory Lectures to the Realm of Absolute Spirit. Ed. J. Glenn Gray. New York: Harper Torchbooks, 1970.

Heidegger, Martin. Kant und das Problem der Metaphysik. Frankfurt am Main, 1965.

Hofstadter, Richard. Anti-Intellectualism in American Life. New York: Vintage Books, 1962.

Husserl, E. Ideas: General Introduction to Pure Phenomenology. Trans. W. R. Boyce Gibson. London: Collier-Macmillan, 1962.

-----. The Crisis of European Sciences and Transcendental Phenomenology. Trans. David Carr. Evanston: Northwestern University Press, 1970.

Hutchinson, Eliot D. How To Think Creatively. New York: Abingdon Press, 1949.

James, William. Principles of Psychology, Vol. II. New York: Henry Holt, 1890.

-----. "The Present Dilemma in Philosophy". In The Writings of William James. Ed. J. J. McDermott. Chicago; London: University of Chicago Press, 1977.

Kant, E. Critique of Pure Reason. Trans. Norman Kemp Smith. New York: St. Martin's Press, 1965.

-----. Logic. Trans. Robert Hartman and Wolfgang Schwarz. Indianapolis: Bobbs-Merrill, 1974.

Kluckhohn, Clyde. "Anthropology in the Twentieth Century". In The Evolution of Science. Eds. Guy S. Metraux and Francois Crouzet. Toronto: The New American Library of Canada Ltd., 1963.

Koch, Adrienne, ed. Philosophy for a Time of Crisis. New York: E. P. Dutton, 1960.

Kroeber, Alfred L., and Clyde Kluckhohn. Culture: A Critical Review of Concepts and Definitions. Harvard University Peabody Museum of American Archeology and Ethnology Papers, Vol. 47, No. 1. Cambridge: The Museum, 1952.

Lefebvre, Henri. The Sociology of Marx. Trans. Norbert Guterman. New York: Vintage Books, 1969.

Lobkowicz, Nicholas. Theory and Practice: History of a Concept from Aristotle to Marx. Notre Dame: University of Notre Dame Press, 1967. Reprinted by UPA in 1983.

Lonergan, Bernard. "Aquinas Today: Tradition and Innovation". The Journal of Religion 55, No. 2 (1975).

-----. A Second Collection. Eds. William Ryan and Bernard Tyrrell. London: Darton, Longman & Todd, 1974.

-----. Collection. Ed. F. E. Crowe. New York: Herder and Herder, 1967.

-----. "Consciousness and the Trinity", unpublished. 1963. The Lonergan Centre, Toronto.

-----. Dublin Lectures on Insight, unpublished. 1961. The Lonergan Centre, Toronto.

-----. Insight: A Study of Human Understanding. New York: Philosophical Library, 1958.

-----. Introduction to Gratia Operans: A Study of the Speculative Development in the Writings of St. Thomas Aquinas, unpublished. Ca. 1943. The Lonergan Centre, Toronto.

-----. Lectures on the Philosophy of Education, unpublished. 1959. The Lonergan Centre, Toronto.

-----. Lecture on the Philosophy of History, unpublished. 1960. The Lonergan Centre, Toronto.

-----. "Merging Horizons: System, Common Sense, Scholarship". Cultural Hermeneutics 1 (1973).

-----. Method in Theology. New York: Herder and Herder, 1972.

-----. "Method: Trend and Variations", unpublished. 1974. The Lonergan Centre, Toronto.

-----. Notes on Existentialism, Thomas More Inst. Typescript, unpublished. 1957. The Lonergan Centre, Toronto.

-----. Notes on Mathematical Logic, unpublished. 1957. The Lonergan Centre, Toronto.

-----. "Theology and Praxis". Address to the Catholic Theological Society of America. 1977.

Lukacs, Georg. History and Class Consciousness. Trans. Rodney Livingstone. Cambridge: The MIT Press, 1971.

Makkreel, Rudolph. Dilthey: Philosopher of the Human Studies. Princeton: Princeton University Press, 1975.

Mannheim, Karl. Ideology and Utopia. Trans. Louis Wirth and Edward Shils. New York: Harcourt, Brace & World, 1936.

Markarian, E. S. "The Concept of Culture in the System of Modern Science". In The Concept and Dynamics of Culture. Ed. Bernardo Bernardi. The Hague: Moulton Publishers, 1977.

Marx, Leo. "Reflections on the Neo-Romantic Critique of Science". Daedalus (Spring 1978).

Maslow, Abraham. The Farther Reaches of Human Nature. New York: The Viking Press, 1972.

-----. The Psychology of Science: A Reconnaissance. Chicago: Henry Regnery Company, 1969.

Mitchell, G. Duncan, ed. A Dictionary of Sociology. London: Routledge & Kegan Paul, 1968.

Molnar, Thomas. The Decline of the Intellectual. New York: Meridian Books, 1961.

Morelli, Elizabeth A., and Mark D. Morelli, eds. Understanding and Being: An Introduction and Companion to Insight. Edwin

Mellen Press, Toronto, 1980.

Mullahy, Patrick. Oedipus: Myth and Complex. New York: Grove Press, 1948.

Murdoch, Iris. The Fire and the Sun, Why Plato Banished the Artists. New York: Oxford University Press, 1978.

Newman, John Henry. A Grammar of Assent. New York: Image Books, 1955.

-----. The Idea of a University. New York: Image Books, 1959.

Nicolson, Sir Harold. Diplomacy. London: Oxford University Press, 1969.

Nzimiro, Ikenna. "Anthropologists and Their Terminologies". In The Concept and Dynamics of Culture. Ed. Bernardo Bernardi. The Hague: Moulton Publishers, 1977.

Ortega y Gasset, Jose. The Revolt of the Masses. Trans. Anon. London: Unwin Books, 1961.

Palmer, Richard E. Hermeneutics. Evanston: Northwestern University Press, 1969.

Parsons, Talcott, et al., eds. Theories of Society: Foundations of Modern Sociological Theory. New York: The Free Press, 1961.

Passmore, John. A Hundred Years of Philosophy. Harmondsworth: Penguin, 1968.

Piaget, Jean. Insights and Illusions of Philosophy. Trans. Wolfe Mays. New York: The World Publ. Company, 1971.

Plato. Republic.

-----. Protagoras.

Price, H. H. "The Appeal to Common Sense". Philosophy 5 (1930).

Radnitzky, Gerard. Contemporary Schools of Metascience. Chicago: Henry Regnery, 1970.

Raitt, A. W. Life and Letters in France, The Nineteenth Century. New York: Scribner's, 1965.

Ramsey, F. P. The Foundations of Mathematics. Ed. R. B. Braithwaite. London: Routledge & Kegan Paul, 1931.

Read, Herbert. _To Hell with Culture_. New York: Schocken Books, 1964.

Rorty, Amelie, ed. _Pragmatic Philosophy_. Garden City: Anchor Books, 1966.

Rorty, Richard. _Consequences of Pragmatism (Essays: 1972-1980)_. Minneapolis: University of Minnesota Press, 1982.

-----. _Philosophy and the Mirror of Nature_. Princeton: Princeton University Press, 1979.

-----, ed. _The Linguistic Turn: Recent Essays in Philosophical Method_. Chicago: University of Chicago Press, 1967.

Rescher, Nicholas. "Philosophical Disagreement". _The Review of Metaphysics_, Vol. XXXII, No. 2 (Dec. 1978).

Sala, Giovanni. "The _A Priori_ in Human Knowledge: Kant's _Critique of Pure Reason_ and Lonergan's _Insight_". _The Thomist_, Vol. XL, No. 2 (1976).

Santayana, George. _The Life of Reason, Vol. I: Reason in Common Sense_. New York: Collier Books, 1962.

Sartre, J.-P. _The Transcendence of the Ego_. Trans. Williams and Kirkpatrick. New York: The Noonday Press, 1957.

Scheler, Max. _Ressentiment_. Trans. William W. Holdheim. New York: Schocken Books, 1972.

Schiller, F. C. S. _Must Philosophers Disagree? And Other Essays in Popular Philosophy_. London: Macmillan, 1934.

Schutz, Alfred. _Collected Papers I: The Problem of Social Reality_. Ed. Maurice Natanson. The Hague: Martinus Nijhoff, 1962.

-----. _Reflections on the Problem of Relevance_. Ed. Richard M. Zaner. New Haven: Yale University Press, 1970.

-----, and Thomas Luckmann. _The Structures of the Life-World_. Trans. Richard M. Zaner and H. Tristram Engelhardt, Jr. Evanston: Northwestern University Press, 1973.

Shorey, Paul. _Platonism Ancient and Modern_. Berkeley: University of California Press, 1938.

Simmel, Georg. _Conflict & The Web of Group-Affiliations_. Trans. Wolff and Bendix. New York: The Free Press, 1955.

Singer, Milton. "The Concept of Culture". In _International Encyclopaedia of the Social Sciences_. Ed. D. L. Sills. New York: Macmillan; The Free Press, 1963.

Smith, John E. _The Spirit of American Philosophy_. Oxford: Oxford University Press, 1963.

Snell, Bruno. _The Discovery of the Mind_. New York: Harper Torchbooks, 1960.

Snow, C. P. _The Two Cultures and the Scientific Revolution_. Cambridge: Cambridge University Press, 1959.

Stegmuller, Wolfgang. _Main Currents in Contemporary German, British, and American Philosophy_. Bloomington: Indiana University Press, 1970.

Sullivan, Harry Stack. _The Interpersonal Theory of Psychiatry_. Eds. Perry and Gawel. New York: W. W. Norton, 1953.

-----. _The Psychiatric Interview_. Eds. Perry and Gawel. New York: W. W. Norton, 1970.

Thevenaz, Pierre. _What is Phenomenology?_ Ed. James Edie. Chicago: Quadrangle Books, 1962.

Thomas Aquinas. _Summa theologiae_ ii, 2, 179.

Tiryakian, Edward A. "Typologies". In _International Encyclopaedia of the Social Sciences_. Ed. D. L. Sills. New York: Macmillan; The Free Press, 1968.

Treves, Marco, and Robert Goldwater, eds. _Artists on Art_. New York: Pantheon Books, 1958. 3rd edition.

Voegelin, Eric. _Order and History, Vol. IV: The Ecumenic Age_. Baton Rouge: Louisiana State Univ. Press, 1974.

-----. "Reason: The Classic Experience". _The Southern Review_ (July 1974).

Wagar, W. Warren. _The City of Man. Prophecies of a World Civilization in Twentieth-Century Thought_. Baltimore: Penguin, 1967.

Weber, Max. _The Theory of Social and Economic Organization_. Trans. and eds. Talcott Parsons and A. M. Henderson. New York: Oxford University Press, 1947.

White, Morton. "Reflections on Anti-intellectualism". _Daedalus_,

Vol. 91, 1962.

-----. _Science and Sentiment in America_. New York: Oxford University Press, 1972.

Winch, Peter. _The Idea of a Social Science and its Relation to Philosophy_. London: Routledge & Kegan Paul, 1963.

Winter, Gibson. _Elements for a Social Ethic_. New York, 1966.